W9-BZV-998

THE nearly departed

OTHER NONFICTION BY BRENDA CULLERTON

Geoffrey Beene: The Anatomy of His Work

A Home for All Seasons

Time at Home

THE nearly departed

or, my family and other foreigners

Brenda Cullerton

Little, Brown and Company
Boston New York London

First Edition
Map illustration by Joel Holland

Grateful acknowledgment is made to the following for permission to reprint previously published material:

Atheneum Books for Young Readers, an imprint of Simon & Schuster Children's Publishing Division from *The Wind in the Willows* by Kenneth Grahame. Copyright 1908, 1937, 1953 Charles Scribner's Sons; copyrights renewed.

Clarkson N. Potter, an imprint of Random House, Inc., for use of a sentence from *The Fearful Void* by Geoffrey Moorhouse.

Library of Congress Cataloging-in-Publication Data

Cullerton, Brenda.
The nearly departed, or, my family and other foreigners / Brenda Cullerton. — 1st ed.
p. cm.
ISBN 0-316-16253-1
1. Cullerton, Brenda — Family. 2. Eccentrics and eccentricities — Connecticut — Ridgefield — Biography. 3. Terminally ill — Family relationships. 4. Adult children — United States — Family relationships. 5. Parent and adult child — United States. 6. Ridgefield (Conn.) — Biography. I. Title: Nearly departed. II. Title: My family and other foreigners. III. Title.

CT9990 .C85 2003
974.6'9 — dc21
[B] 2002034005

10 9 8 7 6 5 4 3 2 1

Q-FF

Book designed by Fearn Cutler de Vicq
Printed in the United States of America

For Richard, Jack, and Nora

"And though it might well be that I should be drawn across the desert by the prospect of an explorer's crown, I also knew that, more powerfully still, I would in truth be propelled by my own fears. . . ."

Geoffrey Moorhouse, *The Fearful Void*

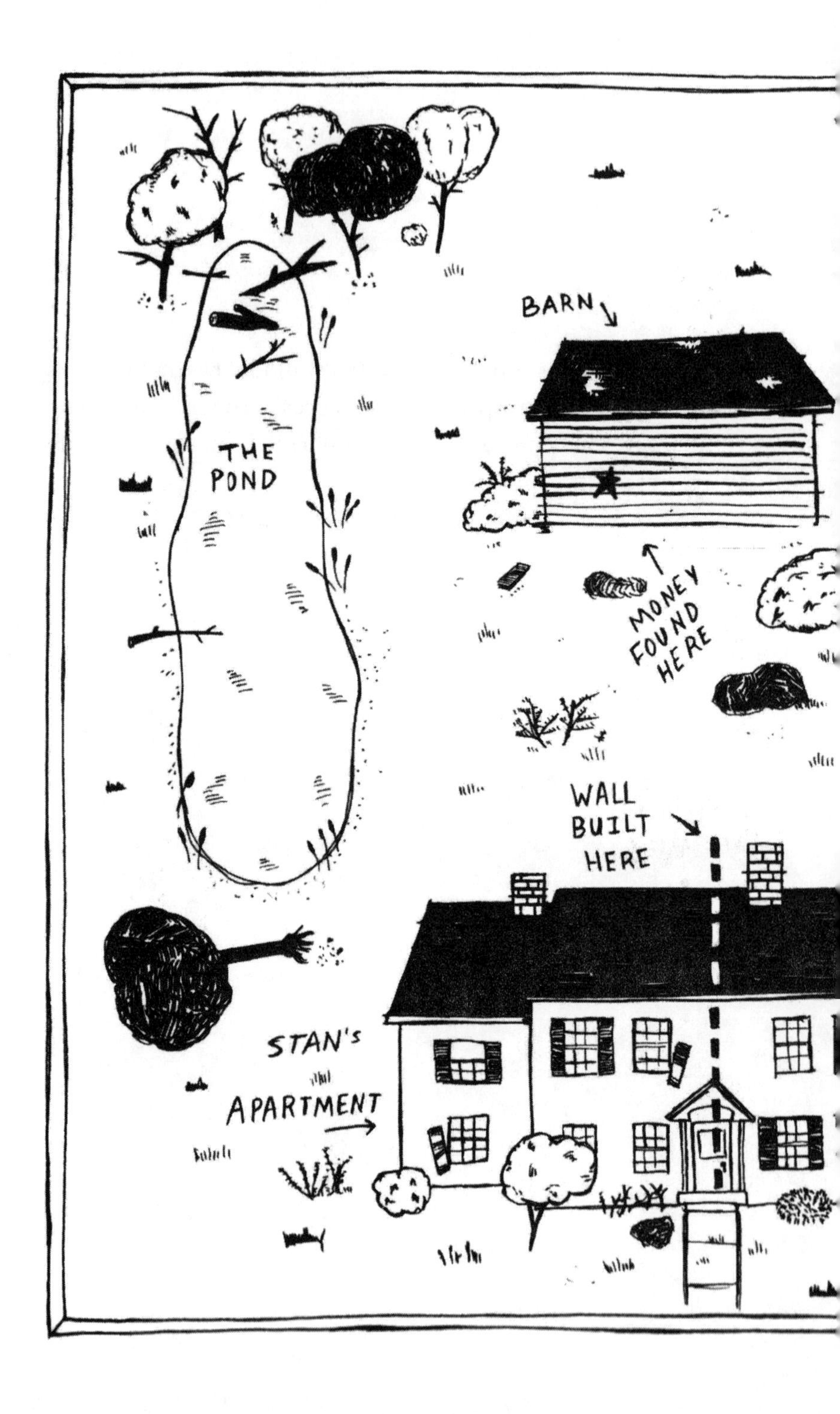

BARN
THE POND
MONEY FOUND HERE
WALL BUILT HERE
STAN's APARTMENT

THE BACKYARD
GEOFF'S TAR-PAPER SHACK
GORDON'S GARDEN
DAD'S HOUSE
MA'S SIDE OF HOUSE

contents

THE nearly departed

FOR THE FIRST TIME IN OVER TWENTY YEARS, MOM'S bedroom windows are open. She's always hated light and air. It's 7:30 on a Saturday morning, and I'm holding her hand. Leaning in to listen to what I keep thinking might be her last words, I can't believe what I hear out in the yard:

"I'll give you four bucks for the lawn chairs."

"Tell you what. Give me six, and I'll throw in the picnic table."

"Deal!"

It's Mother's tenant, Stan — the man who lives on the other side of the wall in her house. He's having a tag sale.

When people say death is difficult to describe or imagine, I don't think this is what they have in mind. With half the town of Ridgefield double-parked on our front lawn and total strangers wandering around our backyard, haggling and hauling away early-bird bargains, I wonder how I could ever have hoped this would be a moment in the life of my family that other human beings could relate to — a moment like in the movies or in novels when children gather quietly around their mother's bedside, weeping and whispering private good-byes.

"What the hell is going on over there?" asks Gail when I pick up the phone. An otherwise unflappable friend and neighbor from across the street, she sounds dumbfounded. "Have you seen the sign at the end of your driveway?"

"Yes, Gail. I've seen it." I'm finally howling, not just with rage and despair but with raucous laughter. My mother's life has been one of such exaggerated horror and humor, the fact her final departure is marked by a huge hand-painted sign outside the house that reads EVERYTHING MUST GO! MOVING SALE! is almost poetic in its perfection.

Steeling myself up to step back into her room, I spray the air around me with essence of lavender, a scent that from now on I will associate only with disguising the smell of death. Mom's mouth is open like a baby bird's, waiting to be fed. Her silver hair, which for years lay hidden beneath a blue cotton bandanna tied like a refugee's beneath her chin, is neatly braided into pigtails. "I don't know where I'm going," she says over and over again. "I don't know where I'm going."

Placing my hands over hers to still her trembling, I dip a cotton ball into a bowl of her favorite Marcus Dairy peppermint-stick ice cream (hand-packed, of course) and squeeze. We've melted the ice cream and mixed it with double her usual dose of Xanax. Without a few drops on her tongue every hour, Mother would suffer the agonies of physical withdrawal. "What irony," I mutter to myself. "And what an absurd and futile gesture." Because it is withdrawal, not from pills or drugs but from the world, that's killed my mother.

seven months earlier…

Mom at nineteen in Danbury, Connecticut

“i have been in tens and tens of houses since aff-rica.”

When the weather’s bad, Mom gets in the car and backs up to visit Dad. It’s about fifty feet in reverse from her house to his, behind the garage. I don’t know which is more dangerous — her driving or her walking. A month ago, she hit a tree. This was right after Christmas. She says it got in the way when she swerved off the road to avoid a jogger. “A jogger with antlers?” asked Eric, my brother’s fifteen-year-old son. Mom has a tendency to “see” things, not just because she wears three pairs of glasses, one on top of the other, but because her vision, her perception of the world, is so brilliantly impaired.

Mother detests joggers. When they first arrived in the neighborhood with their 4 x 4s and custom-built “billion-dollar tract houses,” Mom would follow alongside them in her car, beeping the horn and yelling: “What are you? Nuts? You’re going to die of a heart attack, mister. Go home.” Joggers were put in the same loathsome category as everything else that signified change: chèvre, arugula, color television, even landing on the moon.

"Why would anyone ever want to go to the moon?" This was said with total disdain and amazement at a time when the whole country was euphoric about our conquest of outer space. For the next thirty years, Mom would repeat that same rhetorical question, replacing the word *moon* with *Italy, England, France, Russia, Greenwich* — in short, any destination her children or her husband were headed for that was beyond Ridgefield or Danbury, her hometown, twelve miles away. Mother's mind has always been willing to wander a great deal farther than the rest of her.

These days, I can only imagine the conversations our neighborhood joggers have with their wives. Who is this lunatic? they must wonder when they sprint past our house on the corner. This teeny-tiny woman who, rumor has it, petted and hugged her dog after he bit through the pant leg of her mailman? She was proud of Sandy. He was protecting her. He was heeding "the call of the wild," she said. Mother's entire life has been a call from the wild, a howl from the heart no one could hear. And now, at sixty-eight years old, the wild has finally claimed her.

Unfortunately, her house and all 9.2 acres of our property have gone with her. There's nothing left but the creaking bones of what was once a beautiful old colonial. The wood-shingled roof, soggy from years of snow and rain, has moss growing on it. Vines have crept up the walls and sealed some of the windows shut, and there's a smell in the kitchen that reminds me of the stink you get when you suck between the spaces of a rotten tooth. Eager-beaver Realtors probably assume it's a case of hard times, benign neglect. For those of us closer to the ruins, it's more like Edgar Allan Poe's House of Usher. Mother and the house have become one. Aside from backing up to Dad's and the odd trip into town with Eric, Mom goes nowhere. Confined to a single room off the kitchen and barely able to put one foot in front of the other, she scuttles around sideways, clutching onto everything but straws for support.

As concerned as I am about my mother's deteriorating condition, it is the news about my father that has unexpectedly stunned me. Dad had a massive stroke eighteen years ago. He was fifty-one. But it's his heart and lungs that are finally failing him. Doctors say he has less than four months to live. With the scaly red patches on his face and scalp, the stray silver whiskers that stick out from the spots he misses while shaving, and his stream of obscenities, he too has become part of the wild. A primitive, unyielding force of nature as indomitable as the viselike grip of his left hand. The grip of that hand is still strong enough to break bones. But it is only when my own hand is caught within its grasp that I recognize some small part of the man I once knew as my father.

Dad hasn't had a kind word to say to anyone but the lady who delivers his Meals on Wheels in years. The best thing about his quadruple bypass four years ago was that it proved he still had a heart. We all made jokes about the Tin Man. Then we giggled about Rasputin. Nothing seemed to kill my father off — not strokes or heart attacks, not emphysema or the dozen Hershey bars and handful of Russell Stover chocolate-covered cherries that he devoured every day.

Even his gray wooden cottage behind the garage has become as dark and uninviting as the man who inhabits it. Originally built by Dad's brother, Larry, for their mother after she had her stroke in the early 1970s, it is furnished with bits and pieces of my father's former life as a globe-trotting shoe executive. The green Kermanshah rug from an apartment we owned on Gramercy Park is covered with coffee stains and cigarette burns. There are greasy blue-and-white-striped canvas couches from our old summerhouse on Lake Candlewood and dusty cabinets, full of crystal and china, that haven't been opened since the days when my English grandmother invited us over for afternoon teas.

For years, I have succeeded in maintaining a safe distance between myself and the devastation here in my old backyard. I would drive up to Ridgefield from New York with my husband, Richard, and two children, Jack and Nora, only for the occasional weekend in the summer and fall. These were seasons when sunshine, gentler weather, and the dense overgrowth of foliage helped disguise the extent of the damage. But January is a merciless month, a conspiracy of cold and melting snow that has left both the physical landscape and my own ambivalent feelings about this place I once called home brutally exposed.

If it were only my parents' divided lives and the prospect of their dying that I had to face in the months ahead, I would probably continue to cope the same way that I always have — by wearing emotional Kevlar. But there are others wandering in and around this landscape whose lives leave me feeling so profoundly unsettled that they have taken up residence even in my dreams. There is my uncle Larry, my aunt Janet, my brother, Geoff, and Stan, the man who rents the apartment on the other side of Mother's house. "Reality's refugees," my husband calls them. Driven, possessed, chased, they are unmoored — as unique as they are bereft.

A frequent visitor now that his brother is approaching his final departure, my uncle Larry is seventy-one years old and has been smoking vast amounts of pot for over thirty years. He has never paid federal taxes, worn a watch, or owned a telephone, and he sleeps like a fugitive in the front seat of his gray 1984 Honda with one hand on the steering wheel. With his bushy white beard, missing teeth, and long, unkempt hair tied into a ponytail, Larry could be Hunter Thompson's version of a gonzo Santa Claus. I once thought he was the Unabomber.

Stan, one of Mother's favorite people, is a stunning silver-haired ex-actor. Currently employed as a leisure-furniture salesman, he devotes most of his time to either running errands for Mom in his decrepit red Mazda (the license plates spell DREAMA) or working on his "special projects" on the lawn. His latest project is a half-built wooden bridge, which he intends to hoist from the shore of our pond, across three feet of water, to a tiny island where the skeleton of a weeping willow my father planted when I was young reminds me of the years when this property was the envy of the neighborhood.

My beloved aunt Janet, Mom's younger sister, is a petite blonde who usually arrives just before dark. A lifetime of chain-smoking nonfiltered Camels and basking in the sun while slathered in baby oil and iodine has prematurely aged her. But it was the death of her only son ten years ago that left her truly desolate. Unable to lay his ghost to rest (Mark's ashes are still in a cardboard box in her garage), she has trouble sleeping in her own house in Fairfield. She arrives at dusk in an ancient yellow Datsun and departs shortly after dawn.

My forty-six-year-old brother, Geoff, is the other soon-to-be "permanent" resident. Temporarily camped out at Dad's and separated for the past six years from his wife, Marie, a towering Deneuve-like blonde who became my first best friend in Paris over twenty-six years ago, he is toying with the idea of either moving into a large tent or building himself a tar-paper shack near the barn. The barn, like every other structure in my backyard, is collapsing in on itself. But Geoff is using it to store the remnants of his own previous lives as a shoe designer and traveling salesman. With his gaunt good looks, dark green eyes, and deep throaty laugh, my brother is as handsome, as deliriously seductive and charming, as our father once was. But he is also at his wit's end. And without his wits, without a job, money, or a wife, I worry about what will become of him.

Oddly enough, the only person who appears to be at peace here is Gordon, a young man born in Africa who arrived two weeks ago to help take care of my father. Mother calls Gordon "our man from Ghana." Six foot four with heavily lashed brown eyes and short clipped hair, Gordon is full of optimistic plans to tame the wilderness around him, even to plant a garden in the spring. While I see only the mercilessness of winter and struggle with thoughts of death and disintegration, Gordon sees hope and the possibility of growth. It humbles me, his hope. "I have been in tens and tens of houses since Aff-rica," he recently told me. "All over Conn-ecti-cut. And I have never felt so at home, so com-fort-able." (Gordon pays the same attention to my impossible father as he does to pronouncing his syllables.)

How can this man who still brushes his teeth with a twig and whose face is covered with scars from childhood visits to a tribal witch doctor feel totally at home in my backyard while I, a forty-seven-year-old native and my parents' eldest daughter, feel so out of place? But then again, why shouldn't Gordon feel at home? As far as the rest of the world is concerned, our backyard may as well be Africa. That's how remote and impenetrable, how exotic, it is for anyone who lives with a facade still intact. There's been nothing gradual about the crumbling of our family's facade. It's been falling away in enormous chunks for most of my adult life.

Who would I be without my own facade? I wonder. Without this image of myself that I cultivate as carefully as Gordon plans to cultivate his garden? It is the image of a woman who has known loss but is never at a loss, a woman who can be relied on to hold things together, to keep them whole. This facade and the somewhat conventional life that I lead with my husband and children in New York are part of what makes me such a foreigner here in my own backyard. What frightens me most in gazing out at this half-frozen landscape, littered with rusted-out gutters, broken windowpanes, plastic lawn chairs, and with the ruins of too many lost and luckless lives, is the reminder of just how fragile facade can be.

"chop! chop! wicky! wicky!"

In October, doctors told us that it was osteoporosis. But I believe it's the weight of unshed tears that has collected into the hump that grows on Mother's back. She's lost fifteen pounds in the past three months. If it were only her appetite that had suddenly vanished, I would be less disturbed. Mother has always defined her existence in terms of feast or famine. But it isn't just my mother's appetite. It's everything that once made this five-foot-three-inch woman appear so much larger than the life around her: her voracious curiosity, her humor, her openness.

When Mom went to the doctor, he insisted there was nothing wrong with her, physically, that a good meal and a pair of Easy Spirit shoes wouldn't cure. That appointment was her first since the birth of my sister, Rachel, forty-two years ago, and this time, the doctor wasn't permitted to examine anything above her knees. Perched on the edge of the table and fully clothed, Mom took off like a derailed freight train. "What's this? Paper on the table? What happened to nice old-fashioned cloth? This is what's wrong with the whole medical profession. People should listen to the radio. Nobody needs doctors. Carlton Fredericks. Remember him? He was 'It'! No, put that thing away. [It was a blood-pressure cuff.] Where's your uniform, nurse? What do you mean, you don't have to wear a uniform?"

On and on it went. I ended up shouting out various symptoms to the doctor, which Mother would confirm or deny with a nod of her head. It was the same technique favored by female royalty in the eighteenth century. For them, it was modesty. For Mother, it's a combination of modesty and madness.

She wasn't always this crazy. Just "nervous." And she certainly wasn't modest. Deaf to the sniggers of neighborhood kids, she used to garden in a pair of black baggy underpants and a lace bra, plucking the beetles off rosebushes and belting out songs by Tony Bennett and Johnny Mathis. When I was a kid, music was played at full blast in our house, with every window wide-open. "Ohmigod! I'm exhhhausted!" she'd shriek to the hills. "The heeeat!"

In the small Connecticut town we lived in, where there were hardly any Jews and not a single black, Mother provided the only bit of local color. Trailing along in the wake of her perfume (she wore enough perfume to asphyxiate most household pets), her pop-it beads, and her pink foam curlers, I must have died of embarrassment a million times on Main Street. This was in the early sixties. I was preadolescent. Unlike my younger brother and sister, who never gave a damn about Mother's appearance, I wanted Mom to get her hair "done" at the Paris Salon. (The Paris was named not after the city in France but after Louis Pariscondola, the owner.) I wanted to be a cheerleader. I wanted to "fly up" in the Brownies and wear a little brown beanie.

But according to Mom, it wasn't just the heat that was stifling in Ridgefield or even cigarettes that stunted one's growth. It was everything I dreamed of becoming: a Brownie, a Girl Scout, and a cheerleader. It was also the PTA, the League of Women Voters, country clubs, the Community Center, and Republicans. The list could be as arbitrary as she was. "Mary, Mary, quite contrary," I called her. Anything that smacked of elitism or that involved an organization was off-limits.

The exception was church. Every Sunday, Mother would pull into St. Mary's parking lot, open the door, and with the car still moving, shove us into the arms of the Lord. "Mother, please," I'd whimper, hopping with one foot in and one foot out of the car. "If you don't stop, I'm going to break my ankle."

"Chop! Chop! Wicky! Wicky!" she'd reply, revving the gas. "You're late!" And with that, she was gone in a puff of exhaust.

"Chop! Chop!" was from Charlie Chan. Mom "adored" Charlie Chan. "Wicky! Wicky!" was "Jap" for *hurry up.* "Mr. Moto said it all the time in those marvelous books by Johnny Marquand. He wrote *The Late George Apley.* God, he was a brainy, brainy man. His wife's name was Hooker. I met her through my dear friend Concie. It was Concie who gave me the whole scoop about Stanny White. He was a total voluptuary, had affairs all over the place. But his wife, Bessie, she owned half of Long Island. She was a very devout Catholic."

Unlike Bessie, Mom was a lapsed Catholic. Which probably explains why she kept one foot on the gas in the parking lot. She was afraid He was lying in wait to punish her. For Mother, the fear of God was far from a figure of speech. It was real. But only bank robbers kept the car running like she did. For her, too, the car was a getaway vehicle — a symbol of the little that stood between her and total immobility.

I laugh at the absurdity of those Sundays now that I have two children of my own. What was the point of sending us to church alone when everyone else went to worship together as families? We were in church only to assuage my Mother's guilt. It was fear, not faith, that had us fidgeting with one foot in and one foot out of the pew — the pew farthest from the altar and closest to the exit.

Forty years later, I'm still fidgeting with one foot in and one foot out of the back row of seats everywhere from airplanes and weddings to my children's school plays. This isn't just because I want to be the first one out if the plane crashes or a fire forces everyone to evacuate the chapel and the school gym. It's because I feel I don't belong. Before I became a professional migrant fifteen years ago, I tried working in-house for a number of New York ad agencies and kept an extra coat, purse, and pack of Marlboros in my office. When colleagues came searching for me in the afternoons, they would see the burning butt in the ashtray, the coat on the back of my chair, and the purse in plain sight and automatically assume I'd stepped out for a moment. I had. Not for the bathroom or a creative meeting down the hall but for a matinee in Times Square. In my ten-year career, I must have seen every B movie known to man, including *Mamba* and *Mandingo.* It wasn't getting ahead that motivated me. It was getting out. As a kid, I didn't quite grasp the concept of belonging. No one in the family did. Life was like leaping out of that moving car in the church parking lot. You had to be ready to hit the ground running.

I used to think this was the reason there were so few photographs of us in the house when I was growing up. Because none of us could stand still long enough to pose or to take a picture. But cameras manufacture memories. And the desire to preserve those memories implies that someone will be around long enough to look back at them in the future. Neither of my parents ever had any sense of the future. The future was something that only other people looked forward to.

This is what I think of now when I arrive in my backyard at forty-seven years old, a middle-aged woman. With my father dying in one house and my mother preparing to follow him in another, I think not of their mortality, or even of my own, but of this strange state of futurelessness that has always hung like an invisible shroud over all of us and that continues to define the frenzied, helter-skelter way in which we live our lives.

Perhaps this is why I have been so vigilant, so determined in my efforts to maintain a distance from my family and why I have never really felt at home here. Most families rely on a degree of distance to survive. But not all families define that distance quite so literally. We come from a place where there are no metaphors. Distance, for us, isn't just emotional or metaphorical. It's real. It's as real as the fifty-foot driveway and two different houses that currently keep my parents close but apart. It's as real as the concrete wall Mother built down the middle of the house, twenty-five years ago, when she wasn't getting along with her husband. What others might have seen as our own version of Checkpoint Charlie, Mom envisioned as a perfect solution. This wasn't dividing a house in half. It was keeping a safe distance. With her on one side and Dad on the other, they'd live happily, but separately, ever after.

They certainly did live separately ever after. Dad was away in Europe when the wall went up. From that time on, he pretty much stayed away. Far away. Yet despite the years apart, my parents never bothered to officially separate or divorce. Just like my brother, who moved out of his wife's house six years ago, and my sister, who left her husband five years ago, neither of whom are in a hurry to formally end their marriages. This is the problem with living with one foot in and one foot out. You never really learn how to finish things. Of the three of us kids, only Rachel finished college. She has yet to pick up her diploma. Geoff dropped out of Lake Forest when he was a sophomore, and I left NYU two credits shy of graduation. Even our jobs are open-ended: part-time, short-term, or freelance positions that allow us to go at will. "C'mon! Let's blow this dump," Mom used to say in her fits of restlessness right before restaurants served dessert. Anything in life that implied finality or that shut a door — divorce, diplomas, dessert — instilled panic. Panic is what we mistook for passion. Like passion, panic kept the adrenaline pumping and the pulse racing.

Is it any wonder then that I should feel those same stirrings of restlessness and panic when I see my mother confined to a single room by osteoporosis and by phobias so out of control that nothing seems to contain them, and my father paralyzed, barely able to move or to speak? Their immobility terrifies me. But even when my bags are packed and I have one foot out the door, I realize that, like them, I have nowhere left to run.

"wahoo! wah! the indian will never die!"

THE ONLY CAMERA MY PARENTS EVER OWNED WAS A Polaroid. It was given to my mother by her father as a birthday present when I was a teenager. Most of the images I have of myself as a toddler were passed down to me in the form of stories, which I then "developed" into a series of mental snapshots. One of my favorites is of my brother and me sitting cross-legged in a sandbox, surrounded by a heap of shining silver. A friend of Mom's looks down at us, her mouth open in a perfect O of shock, as we savagely scratch away at the bright, polished surfaces of gravy boats, water pitchers, and cake platters. Apparently, when Dad later asked my mother what in hell she thought she was doing, letting us play with sterling silver in a sandbox, Mom told him that sand kept the tarnish off.

In another favorite snapshot, Mom is perched on a brown velvet couch, fiddling with her one hoop earring. I'm curled up next to her, grinning, with a copy of *The Gingerbread Man* on my lap. The hem of her faded flower-power sundress has been shortened not with a needle and thread but with a row of giant safety pins. Mom had memorized *The Gingerbread Man* and raced through the story almost as quickly as the main character ran away from little boys, old men, farmers, and wolves. In the last scene, when the fox was about to eat the Gingerbread Man, she would jump up from the couch, pins popping, and shout, "SNIP SNAP. He opened his mouth, and that was the end of the Gingerbread Man."

It didn't take Sherlock Holmes or Freud to figure out why Mom knew *The Gingerbread Man* by heart. It was the story of her life. Mom ran away from everyone. She ran away from her father, her sisters, her friends, her children. She ran away from the sad and the sick, from pain, doubt, despair, and desire. She confused the vehemence of her opinions with emotions. Emotions, like her famous chocolate wafer icebox cake, were too rich to dole out or digest in more than tiny slivers. "There's enough on that plate for the Russian Army," she'd say, pointing at our meager ration of cake. "Eat any more and you'd have to be hospitalized!" The best part of this chocolate wafer icebox cake for us was the fact that it didn't involve any cooking. Mom had no time for cooking. She had to keep moving so the demons wouldn't catch her.

As age slowed my mother down and the distance between her and the demons diminished, her desperate need to keep moving grew more and more exaggerated. Before her fears of fire and derailment in the Park Avenue tunnel ended her trips to New York twelve years ago, she'd come in to visit me but refuse to venture any farther from the reassuring rumble of arriving and departing trains than the lobby of the Grand Hyatt or the Oyster Bar. There, minutes from the track, she'd nurse a cup of coffee or eat her oyster pan roast, and wait for a chat.

"Hey, Mom," I'd say, giving her a kiss and settling in beside her. "Why don't you come down and see the apartment today?" Mother had only seen my apartment in photographs.

"It's too far."

"It's twenty blocks, Ma. We'll take a taxi."

"Ha! A taxi?" she'd say with a snort of total disbelief. "Are you insane? No one takes taxis in this town anymore."

The diatribe that followed — reports of "Cossack cabbies" mowing down pedestrians "willy-nilly" and "gouging" tourists at airports — made the notion of hailing a cab in New York sound as deranged as sailing around Cape Horn in a Sunfish. I didn't take it personally, this reluctance to leave the station and visit the apartment in the West Village where I was living with my husband and newborn son, Jack. I understood the restlessness and the fears. I also knew that, like a blind woman, Mother could only function within the parameters of an intimately familiar world — a world in which everything from objects to opinions remained firmly in place. An hour after I'd ordered my coffee, we would walk together to the gate, and I would put her safely aboard the 4:07 to New Canaan. New Canaan was the closest train station to Ridgefield. It's where Mother parked her car.

Throughout the past year, the car has become Mother's last refuge, a world she's made her own with piles of old down pillows, overdue library books, and ratty wool blankets. No longer reassured by leaving the keys in the ignition with the engine idling while dashing into stores or inhaling her breakfast at the local diner, Mom seemed to prefer not to get out of her car at all. In the spring, she started driving up and parking behind the catcher to watch her grandson Eric's baseball games. Everybody else, of course, was in the bleachers. Far from embarrassed, Eric, the star of the team, would wave to her from the pitcher's mound. That wave seemed heroic to me — a sign that this gentle adolescent boy didn't just accept my mother's eccentricities, he embraced them. When Eric pitched a strike, Mom would stick her head out of the car window, beep the horn, and holler: "Bully! Bully! Bunnie. Bully! Bully!" "Bully! Bully!" was an homage to Teddy Roosevelt, one of Mom's many dead male heroes.

She then buried herself in the pages of the *New York Post.* Her defection from the *New York Times* ("Don't talk to me about that dumbed-down paper, that rag. They should be ashamed of themselves.") and her alliance with Barney, the purple dinosaur, may have also been symptoms of the coming cataclysm.

Once upon a time, Barney's perpetual perkiness would have prompted comments like "That dinosaur should be shot. What a travesty." It was amazing how many people Mother also wanted shot: rude train conductors, bad teachers, bank tellers who had the temerity to suggest she might be overdrawn. Now her only objection seemed to be the color of Barney's skin.

"I kept telling the lady at Caldor's she was wrong. Barney isn't purple. I've seen him on television. He's as black as the hole of Calcutta."

"That's because you watch him on a black-and-white TV, Mom."

"Oh," was all she said. "Well, that's just one more reason not to own a color television. Who ever heard of a purple dinosaur?"

If it wasn't for her bitching about not getting a Mother's Day card, we might have overlooked her crush on Barney. After all, this was a woman who had taught us to despise "crass commercialism." A "Hellmarked" culture. Yet here she was veering toward the Right. I don't mean in the car. Her vital signs were fading: the vividness of her opinions, that relentless questioning of everyone from plumbers and garbagemen to elementary school students, was giving way to cantankerous intolerance. Even in the occasional moments over the past year when she resembled the woman I knew, it was like talking to some lousy impersonator — someone who had rehearsed a few of her most memorable lines and gestures but who was missing the essence of her character.

Her last stand before the appointment with the doctor in October was on behalf of her beloved Indians and against the use of "dirty words" like *indigenous peoples* and *Native Americans.*

"You think Hiawatha and Sacagawea want to be called *indigenous peoples?*" she huffed and puffed while plastering a bumper sticker on the back window of her car. "Wahoo! Wah! The Indian Will Never Die!" it said. She'd ordered it from the *Dartmouth Newsletter.* Mom flung around the intimate details of Indians' lives the way *People* magazine gossips about Calvin and Madonna. According to Mother, she had "discovered" the Indians.

It seems one of her many heroes, Sam Houston, had fallen in love with and left his wife for an Apache. "He never did disclose why he divorced," she told me in the hushed tones used by those privy to insider information. "Only a few of us know the real reason why." She then segued into a monologue about Santa Anna: "I just can't believe you've never heard of him. I adored him. He was that big-time Mexican. Verrry uppercase." And in yet another of her many conversational derailments, "I went to school with the president of Mexico's granddaughter. Madera was her name. The grandfather got bumped off, naturally. Mexicans are good at that — bumping people off. She was divine, though. Now there was class. I'd never want to *go* to Mexico, of course. But I'm fascinated by it."

The president of Mexico, Sam Houston, Santa Anna. Mom was a bosom buddy of everyone she admired. Dead or alive. A hopeless snob, she dropped names the same way she did curlers. (When we were kids, people were always running up to us at the Grand Union with the handfuls of curlers they found near the checkout counter. The boredom of standing in line had her pulling her hair out.) If she hadn't actually gone to school or camp with a daughter, a first cousin once removed, or a friend of the family like Concie, she'd read every word ever written about them. But the fact that she spoke with the same enthusiasm about "big muckety-mucks" like Stanny White, Johnny Marquand, and the president of Mexico as she did about Joey McGowan, "the most famous plumber in Danbury," somehow took the sting out of her snobbery.

She was a woman no impersonator could ever hope to mimic. But her heart no longer had the strength to howl. When kids teased her about the "Wahoo! Wah!" in October, there were no tirades. She sniffed and turned away. Mom was just going through the motions. It was life, not the snip-snap jaws of death, that had finally caught up with her. Not even ten milligrams of Paxil and five Xanax a day now keep those demons at bay. Her hands tremble, and her eyes are filled with tears. Yet I am as stingy with my sympathy as she once was with her smidgens of icebox cake.

But I still refuse to believe that Mother has decided to stop eating and starve herself to death. Like her own bones, words seem to lack any real mass or density when it comes to describing my mother. Her fear of dying has haunted her since childhood. So much so, that we as a family hardly ever acknowledge the "passing" of loved ones: aunts, cats, dogs, grandmothers, great-aunts. They all just up and disappear without a trace.

For us, death is a lot like checking into an airport. We don't expect anyone there at the gate to see us off or to wave farewell. We travel into the afterlife as casually as we do everywhere else. When my aunt Janet returned home from thirty days in a New York rehab clinic in 1988 and found her son, our first cousin Mark, dead of a drug overdose on her kitchen floor, his death prompted nothing more from us than a few commiserating phone calls. There was no funeral or memorial service, no parting words to accompany him on his final journey. "Now you see us; now you don't." This has always been our modus operandi. But seeing my mother disappear before my very eyes is like being forced to watch a child drown. "I wish I could slap myself. Snap out of it," she says between sobs. "I wish it was how it used to be."

"I guess I've become a bit agoraphobic," she adds, lighting her zillionth "OP" ("Other People's" cigarettes). "You guess? A bit?" I whisper to myself, staring at the bedroom walls papered with *National Geographic* maps. My mind, like hers, is definitely wandering. I'm thinking of all the places I've been, the years and years of travel. It was fear that first fooled me into thinking I was brave enough to leave my backyard behind and see the world. It's fear that now fools me into thinking I'm brave enough to stay put and look back.

"terror is your family crest."

I WAS ELEVEN WHEN I LEFT HOME FOR THE CONVENT OF the Sacred Heart, a boarding school in Albany, New York. The only time I ever recall feeling even remotely homesick was during the Cuban missile crisis. With no television or newspapers, I'm not sure how the anxiety that had an entire nation holding its breath also managed to seep through the thick stone walls of the convent and infect a boisterous group of prepubescent girls with sudden fears about the end of the world. But for three nights, we tiptoed nervously around the dormitory after lights-out, trading holy cards and sharing our fears over secret stashes of melted Mallo Cups. I still get cravings for the comforting mouthfuls of shredded coconut, creamy marshmallow, and chocolate.

During those formative years, I had very little contact with my brother or my sister. On my rare visits home, they called me Queenie. So did Mom. Even my summer vacations were spent away from home. In July, I worked as a mother's helper for friends of my parents in New York. In August, I flew down to stay with a convent friend named Cecilia in Caracas. Caracas was the city where I first fell in love with a boy (his name was Juan Andres Vegas) and with the sound of another language. When I returned to Ridgefield, I'd shut myself up in my bedroom with a pack of Benson & Hedges 100's and cry inconsolably, thinking of the boy and the real home I'd left behind.

It was only my father who was able to reach me when I withdrew into my room to relive those weeks of happiness that I had experienced so far away. I identified with Dad. Like me, he was hardly ever home. His job as president of Clarks of England, a British shoe company, kept him on the road and in the air for months. And like me, he was always arguing with Mother. "Just try talking with your brother and sister," he'd whisper, sitting on the floor next to my bed and gently rubbing my back. "You might enjoy their company." But what did I, a teenager dressed in my matching outfits of wool kilts, vests, and brown brogues, pining away for a dark-eyed Venezuelan poet, have in common with a sister who walked around the halls of a public school wearing her father's shirts and pants, or with a longhaired hippie brother who read Eldridge Cleaver and dreamed of growing an Afro.

Whatever comfort I had found in devouring my Mallo Cups at midnight in the convent was long gone by the time I suffered my first full-fledged panic attack at eighteen. The attack seemed to come out of nowhere, and from the moment the symptoms surfaced — the accelerated heartbeat, the sweaty palms and dizziness — I thought I was dying. "I've set up an appointment with John Brooke in New York," Mom quietly informed me. "I think you'll like him."

John Brooke was Mother's occasional shrink, a roly-poly man with a head of curly black hair. Mother told me that he had been crippled by polio in his youth. As I wriggled around in a chrome-and-leather chair in his Upper West Side basement office, I tried desperately not to stare at his withered, shrunken legs. Even his feet looked broken. "Terror is your family crest" were his opening words. The only thing I could think of was the Pan Am ticket Dad had given me for Christmas. "Valid anytime except this afternoon," he'd written on the card. All I had to do was fill in the blank. Who in God's name would choose to stay here? I wondered, and talk about terror and the tedious terrain of their own backyard, when they could be trekking over the Khyber Pass or freighter-hitching in the South Seas?

Off I went with my ticket to Ireland, alone and in the dead of winter. From Ireland, it was on to France, where I'd arranged to do a spring semester at the Sorbonne. That one semester abroad when I was eighteen would not only stretch into over two years away without a single visit home but into a lifetime of commuting back and forth to Europe. Throughout those years, I smirked at those who set up shrines with souvenirs from home, who carried snapshots in their wallets and brought back slides to show their friends and family. I preferred the life of a sleeper. In the days before terrorism, sleepers were specially trained foreign agents. Planted in the heart of enemy territory and cut off from all contact with the familiar, they penetrated through assimilation — by slipping in and out of other people's skins. Frequently indistinguishable from the natives who surrounded them, the sleeper knew there was no such thing as a foreigner. Everyone was a foreigner.

"Why don't you come home, dear?" my father suggested. "Get to know your family before it's too late?" The two of us were drinking a blanc de blanc in the lobby of the Hotel Meurice in Paris. I was twenty-one. They felt almost illicit — these brief hotel encounters with my father. He would fly into Paris every couple of months from Italy or Spain, rent us a magnificent two-bedroom suite for the night, and treat me to dinner. On the afternoon we met at the Meurice, an enormously fat Greek sat sprawled on a delicate red-velvet love seat across from us in the lobby. He was so short, his feet barely touched the ground. With his moss-green silk shirt stretched tight over ripples of flesh and his bulging, sunken eyes, he reminded us of Mr. Toad from *The Wind in the Willows.* Three days later, I was on a plane with Dad, heading home.

In my ten years away, I had become a pro at fitting into the tight, untidy spaces of other people's lives. In assuming it was more important to understand than to be understood, I developed a great "ear." I learned to listen. Sometimes, I identified so closely with other people's languages, I really did feel as if I had slipped into their skin. Disappearing into other people's lives, being a sleeper, kept me safe. There was less danger of being exposed.

But I'd never learned how to inhabit rather than merely occupy a room. I owned no personal possessions, nothing that might give me away. Suddenly, here I was at home feeling like a stranded tourist. Who were these far-from-perfect strangers? For two months after that first return from Europe, I refused to unpack my suitcases. They sat next to my bed and just within reach, a reminder that I would soon be off and running. But in all the years of running, it was the departure, not the destination, that moved me. Unlike those who hurried across the no-man's-land of ocean and space separating one point from another, I took my time on ships and trains. I felt safe within the confines of those small self-contained rooms where everything had its place. The sink and tiny shower, the single set of drawers, the berth or bunk. Leaving, disappearing . . . feeling those first fetal-like kicks of freedom and fear as the familiar slipped away. God, how I loved distance and motion.

With very few exceptions — Paris, London, Hong Kong — my most passionate memories are of those moments stepping aboard Greek and Swedish ferries, Turkish freighters, old transatlantic liners, and trains: the Venice Simplon, the Trans-Siberian, the Orient Express. Reassured by the monotony of movement, I felt the euphoria of rootlessness. I had no idea then that I had inherited my mother's phobias. I only knew that the sight of land or the voice of a conductor announcing the final stop made my palms sweat and my heart flutter. While everyone else was caught up in the exhilaration of last-minute packing and looking forward to setting both feet on the ground, I was dragging my heels. Sometimes, the sensation of lethargy was so intense, my legs felt heavy, as if they had to push their way through water. Now it's Mother who complains of this heaviness in her legs. Her legs are as thin as a cricket's. But the impulse to run still has her lying down and sleeping with one foot on and one foot off the bed. It's involuntary, a reflex. She doesn't even know she's doing it.

"Please get me out of this house," she pleads, her fingers worrying the frayed tassels of her hand-knit purple afghan.

This is the first weekday visit that I have made up to Ridgefield in years. I've come up by train from Grand Central with the halfhearted hope that I can help Geoff coerce Mom into getting fitted for a back brace. While I'm in the kitchen mopping up the blizzard of baking soda and coffee grounds on the counter (Mother insists this is the only healthy way to get rid of ants, but how many ants can there be at the end of February?), I hear her whispering in the bedroom.

"Who's there? Who's that?"

"It's OK, Mom; it's me. It's only me."

"Did you double lock the doors and close the windows? Could you check again? I feel a draft."

It's the panic, the urgency in her voice, that sends me hurrying in to reassure her. "Someone's in the kitchen," she says. "I heard footsteps. I heard them coming through the door." This house, once Mom's sanctuary, is so alive with menace, it's literally scaring her to death. But even when Mom was brave enough to leave her bed and close the windows or to investigate such noises, she was so afraid to make her presence known, to alert whatever lay waiting for her in the shadows, that she'd tiptoe like a trespasser across the floor.

Mother hasn't been up the stairs or across the wall to the other side of her own house since 1989. "Aren't you even curious?" I shout out from the kitchen. I'm checking the expiration dates on cereal boxes. Mom only throws out important stuff like bills and bank statements. Everything else from magazines to frozen peas and cereal dates back at least five years.

"What's to see?" she says impatiently. "I'm sure it all looks exactly the same, and I do have Susan." Susan is Mom's very depressed but devoted cleaning woman. She changes the sheets once a week and vacuums.

It's the emptiness and the vacancy that terrifies her. For years, Mother ran our house like a suburban refugee camp. I'd arrive for holiday visits from school and find milk and yogurt cartons in the refrigerator taped with names of strangers like *Kenny* and *Sam* and my closets crammed with their clothing. "Someone's been sleeping in my bed," I'd joke. Near and very distant relatives, friends of friends, neighbors' kids . . . people seemed to come from miles around to stay at Mother's place. She loved the company. But all that's left now of Mother's guests are ghosts. Perhaps these are the footsteps she hears as she lies as stiff and wary as a sentinel in her bed.

Last fall, my husband told her we were planning to rent a Winnebago for our next trip up and gave her a MasterCard sticker for the back door. Mother laughed so hard, she almost fell over. But when I saw him glue the MasterCard sticker on Mother's door, I realized that there was only one problem with this endless parade of people passing though my house, with all this coming in and going out. It made our house a home for all but those who belonged there. Us. There was no room for us.

"i'm a cripple. i'm entitled."

JUDGING FROM GEOFF'S TAR-PAPER SHACK NEAR THE BARN, there still isn't room for us. Talk about one foot in and one foot out. You can't get much more out than a tar-paper shack. Except for a tent, which was his original plan. On the dreary March morning when we pull into the driveway in the pouring rain and I see my brother putting the finishing touches on his shack, I am livid with rage. But I am also laughing. For years, I've been struggling to get out from beneath this burden of anger and affection, this furious love, that I feel for my brother.

Too long ago forgotten by our father and too easily forgiven by our mother, Geoff can be as gentle as Jesus. I once thought he had the hands, the touch, of a true healer. But he is also a man who sometimes appears to have no conscience at all. Much as I yearn to believe in him, I am always wary of his motives. "No way I'm buying it," I'd said to him on the night he called me to "discuss" the tent. "Don't even waste your time trying to talk me into it. It's deranged." But Geoff, like our father, was born a salesman. And born salesmen are bulletproof and blind to everyone's viewpoint but their own.

"Think of the tent as a kind of low overhead, Bren."

"Very funny, Geoff."

"Look," he said, suddenly changing tack, "the truth is, I want to be close to Mom and Dad. They need me here."

I am not the first person to kid myself into thinking that I am immune to my brother's powers, that in knowing just how dangerous and mesmerizing he can be, I am better able to resist him. But the fact is, I have no memory of the conversation that followed. Twenty minutes after saying "no way" to Geoff, I have not only succumbed to the absurdity of his plan, I am more enthusiastic about it than he is.

"How 'bout something cozy in canvas?" I say. "Like Peter Beard's tent in Kenya, with little touches of luxury like threadbare Orientals, pillows, kerosene lamps. Or maybe one of those cabanas built for medieval jousting tournaments."

"Oh, yeah. I can see it perfectly," Geoff replies. "All candy-colored stripes with flags and pennants flying. People might think we're throwing a party."

Instead what we've got is this one-room tar-paper shack with a single bed, a Bunsen burner, and a three-foot plastic duck outside the door. With the disemboweled 1982 Le Car, the Chrysler LeBaron, and the three-wheeled RV, which Uncle Larry plans to drive up to Nome, Alaska, when he finds a fourth wheel, our backyard is beginning to look like a tiny piece of Appalachia, what Southerners call a genuine "haller."

It's Uncle Larry who helped Geoff build his shack. When I

catch a glimpse of him trotting out from behind the barn with a seat belt around his waist (he uses it to hold his tools) and tugging at his beard, I wish my uncle were anywhere but here. Larry has just resurfaced after a week of partying underground. Twice a year, he and a bunch of bluegrass-loving buddies descend into an abandoned coal mine somewhere down in Pennsylvania. My *Satyricon*-like visions of them dancing to the strains of frenzied fiddling and blowing dope in the bowels of the earth makes my hair stand on end. When Larry isn't on the road partying or sleeping with one hand on the steering wheel of his Honda in our driveway, he lives in his own rundown shack on the otherwise scenic shores of Lake Pruit in northern Connecticut. One of several ad hoc structures located on his twelve-acre self-styled "commune," the shack has no electricity or heat. Holes in the roof and walls are plugged up with balls of twenty-year-old newspapers. Amazingly enough, Larry went to Yale, where he majored in architecture, and is a fine builder — but only of other people's houses.

As a kid, I loved my uncle Larry. As a "grown-up," I love him less. At yet another time in my brother's life when he could desperately use an adult's guidance, my seventy-one-year-old uncle just wants to get stoned. And I don't want Geoff to end up like Larry, a pothead with nowhere to sleep but the front seat of a car or the back of a clapped-out van, a drifter with ties to no one but his children. For the moment, it is only Geoff's love for these children — Eric, Nate, and Madeleine — that slows him down and keeps him grounded.

Geoff's teenage kids, Nate and Eric, are in their clubhouse in the barn. I can hear Jimi Hendrix blaring through what's left of the windows. What the hell do they make of all this? I wonder. Of their loony great-uncle Larry? of their forty-six-year-old father moving into a shack in his parents' yard? of a grandmother confined to quarters, sharing her house with a series of flaky tenants like Stan and her sister Janet? And what about their grandfather? Even today, my idea of the perfect grandfather is the benevolent, loving old man in *Heidi.* It is not a man who between huge gulps of oxygen and Hershey bars greets his grandchildren with a string of four-letter words that would make an urban rapper blush.

"Bastard! Fuck! Son of a bitch!" There are moments I catch myself listening to my father and realize it isn't just his memory that's gone. It's mine. Who is this swearing 250-pound cripple who thinks he's so entitled? "I'm a cripple. I'm entitled" is Dad's mantra. He's repeated it so often over the years, the lady from Meals on Wheels had it embroidered on a sampler that hangs over the kitchen table. She also made him a pillow for the couch that says "It's Hard to Be Humble When You're from Dartmouth!"

Before his stroke eighteen years ago, Dad was a man whose spare, careful use of words gave him a power I associated with prophets and oracles, a man whose friends said should have been a poet, not a businessman. It was Dad's gentle words that had seduced me into speaking when I had withdrawn behind my wall of silence as a kid. And it was his talks that had also reassured me in my first mute and friendless months abroad. "The only thing in life worth accumulating is experience," he'd told me, while trying to nurse a single Scotch in the lobby of the old Hibernian in Dublin. "And the best experiences begin with feeling uncomfortable."

I could never picture my father uncomfortable until he had

his stroke. He had been a master of ease and of fluency: as eloquent when he taught me how to swim as he was when he danced, or flew across the ice and showed me how to skate with two hands clasped behind my back. Like Mother and his brother, Larry, Dad was always on the move. He couldn't bear standing still.

The difference was that, over the years, Dad moved farther and farther away. As the president of Clarks of England, he introduced America to the Desert boot and the Wallabee. The more successful Dad became, the less we saw him. His presence at home was reduced to a series of cameo appearances punctuated by the occasional postcard, telex, or phone call from Rome, London, Florence, or Geneva. But like God the Father Almighty, I didn't need to see him to believe in him.

The stroke didn't just clip my father's wings at fifty-one years old — it cut them off. That this should have been what sobered him up and eventually brought him "home" to his wife is almost as twisted as *Ethan Frome.* Wharton's novel is one of Mother's favorites. Only I see the parallel between herself as Zeena, the wife, and the fate of her husband and his lover, who, dreaming of escape from her on a moonlight sleigh ride, end up crippled and dependent upon her for the rest of their days instead.

It was Mother who found Dad at our summerhouse after he'd had the stroke in 1980. By then, the distance that separated my parents had expanded far beyond the wall down the middle of Mother's house. Dad was drinking, had been fired from Clarks, and was camping like a gypsy at the house on Lake Candlewood. When Dad arrived by ambulance at the hospital, doctors told Mother that he had probably had the stroke more than twelve hours before she discovered him. They also told her that he had been badly beaten.

I had idolized my father when I was growing up. He was what I'd dreamed of becoming: an adult. He was the man who'd taught me to swim and to skate, who'd run into a swarm of furious mud wasps and picked me up his arms after I'd stuck my finger down the hole of their nest while playing in the driveway, and who'd packed me in a pit of cold mud to soothe away the pain of the stings. As the oldest child (I was 29) and his closest ally, it seemed only natural that I become the conservator of his person and estate.

Earning an annual income of $32,000 and still filing my tax returns with H&R Block, I knew as much about finances as Marie Antoinette knew about farming. Sure, I had my job as a copywriter in advertising. But like the queen on her weekend jaunts to the dairy barn, I was just pretending. The jobs were a means to save enough money to keep on running. If the money ran out, Dad had always come to the rescue. Now he was in rehab singing "Row, Row, Row Your Boat," and I was bailing out a ship so full of holes that I'm still not sure how I kept our heads above water.

"Liquidate; liquidate everything," advised his accountants. But Dad had already done that, drinking Rob Roys and neat Dewar's everywhere from the Rusty Nail in Ridgefield to the Savoy in London. Most of what was left was in what you might call "hidden assets." They were so hidden that Dad was in the hospital scrawling pirate maps on napkins with squiggly *x*'s on them. Richard and I finally figured out they were maps of the inside of our barn. For three weekends, we rootled around through bat shit and shoe boxes in search of treasure. The boxes were full of moldy shoe samples. After Clarks fired him, Dad opened a new company called EconShu, which promptly failed. Wads of cash were crinkled up like tissue paper in the toes of the shoes.

Then there were the loans to "friends" in town: forty grand to a guy who dreamed of opening a video store in Boston, thirty more to a buddy on the run from credit card companies, three hundred thousand to a local builder strapped for cash. The builder set up our rendezvous in the Grand Union parking lot, where he handed over interest payments stuffed into shopping bags. Ten thousand dollars in small notes fills up a lot of bags.

Until the stroke, I never had to ask for anything. Overnight, I became the repo man, forced to knock on strangers' doors on Sunday mornings and beg full-grown men to cough up what they owed us. I remember the collapsed look on the wives' faces, the humiliated shuffle of slippers as they went to fetch their husbands and tried to herd their inquisitive children out of earshot.

I'd always assumed my father was watching over me. How could he sink thousands of dollars into oil wells with a drunken dentist? Drilling into molars is one thing, the earth another. And the real estate . . . he dropped his entire golden parachute on top of a mountain. "I'm not doing this for you," I remember him telling me. "I'm doing it for your children."

It was a housing development called Parkwood that made a fortune for everyone but us — for the banks that charged 18 percent on the loan, for the companies that had to dig the wells and build the roads and install the central-vacuum and air-conditioning systems. We went into foreclosure after I'd squirreled away $3,000 from the sale of two bulldozers. Dick Mahoney, the guy who pitched the deal to my father, was a philatelist who moonlighted as a used car salesman. Last I heard, he'd been arrested for embezzlement in Australia.

The bottom line is that for a man who had been totally inaccessible to those who loved him most, my father sure was accessible to everyone else. And they took him for every cent he had. This was the saddest, most unbearable part of it all for me. Equally unbearable was the fact that I had no chance to mourn his loss. Overnight, there just became less of him. A lot less.

Money, for me, was the least of those losses. Dad had never been mean. Not with money, anyway. It wasn't even the loss of his power of speech or of physical movement that so diminished him in my eyes. It was the lightning-like loss of my own faith and innocence. If Mother was transparently obvious, Dad was opaque. He was never what he seemed. This wasn't necessarily a bad thing. It was even generous in its way. But it was distance, not proximity, that had kept us so close and that defined his romance and power.

Accountants told me that in the 1970s Dad was making a million dollars a year — more money than the chairman of General Motors. But his losing streak was as spectacular as his rise. It wasn't just his job or the money he threw away. Dad was a man who never had to raise his voice to be heard. Drinking made him loud. The stealthlike humor, the light, deft touch, that made everyone so eager to please him, gave way to a heavy-handed coarseness, a vulgarity, that made me cringe.

Everything about my father, including his arteries, now seems to have hardened. He's petrified not with fear like

Mother but like a fossil. Even his routine is as inflexible as his atrophied muscles. (Eight years ago, he started renting videos that began with the letter *a*. He's up to *m* today.) The precise placement of his chair, his books — one on African mammals, the other on Irish castles — and his favorite ashtray from the Hassler in Rome (yes, we all smoke despite the oxygen tanks) is absolute. It never varies. The yellow legal pads on which he made the lists that ruled our lives are covered with childish drawings of lightbulbs, pill bottles, and ice cream cartons, another haunting piece of debris left in the wake of his aborted departure.

All that remains of my father is his will to live and his fear of loss, both of which seem to have come a little late. This is what his inability to give, the miserliness with his possessions, the hoarding of money, is about. There are glimmers of the glamour I remember, of the grace and suppleness that propelled him not just across the ice and water but through life. There is even bravery. But when I hear his disembodied voice on my answering machine, repeating his own name over and over again, "Bob Cullerton. Bob Cullerton," I press Skip and Delete. It is as if in pushing these buttons, I will obliterate the reminder of a man who, far from watching over me, chose to forget all about me instead. This is what I've always done in order to survive: skip, delete, erase, escape. It's the only way I know how to keep going.

"i am a stubborn prick."

"I'M TELLING YOU, THEY WERE DROOLING DOWN AT KINney's." Kinney's is our local garage in the Village, and Richard is crowing as we cruise up the Sawmill River Parkway in his new electric-blue Lexus. "It's a guy magnet," he says, pushing a button on the steering wheel that somehow controls the volume on his CD player. "Cool, huh?" Until now, the day before St. Patrick's Day and our maiden voyage in the Lexus, I hated shiny show-off cars like this. But after zipping by the Spuyten Duyvil tollbooth with our E-ZPass, over the Hudson, and past a parade of Orthodox Jews slowly marching single file toward their temple in Riverdale, I am lulled into a luxurious stupor. There is no sensation of speed in this car, no bumps, no sounds from the engine. With the forlorn, hypnotic voice of singer Andy Bey in the CD player and with exit signs for Chappaqua and Mt. Kisco soon drifting into the distance behind us, I feel as if I am being gently lured, not driven, toward Connecticut.

As we glide into the space next to Mother's Oldsmobile, Gordon is already standing there, waiting for us. It unnerves me, this uncanny knack he has of suddenly appearing and disappearing. I'm not quite sure how he does it. Holding his gardening machete in one hand, he opens my door with the other and grins. "How are you fitting in up here in the land of the crazy white man?" I ask him. "I do not want to leave," he says, his eyes caressing the car. "My wife, she misses me. I don't call home like other jobs. I am happy."

It must be culture shock, the head-spinning dizziness and exhaustion I so often experience when I get out of the car here. Four hours ago, I was thirty-two floors above the street, pitching a slogan to a group of high-powered females in suits. The slogan — "MAKE UP. YOUR MIND" — was for a new line of "fun, youth-oriented cosmetics." Now I'm casually chitchatting with an African wielding a machete.

Clients like to think I "develop" these slogans in focus groups and through market research. But the best ones usually emerge while I'm soaking in a hot tub with a cold martini: "LET GO. AND LIFE BEGINS AGAIN" for Zelda; "FIT IN. STAND OUT" for Hanes; "LET HER BE" for Anne Klein. They're distillations of my own experience, of hidden hopes and longings. They're all about what's personal and pure projection. But how can I continue to reduce the essence of my own experience into three- and four-word slogans when my life is becoming so estranged from the world outside it?

"C'mon," says Gordon, grabbing my arm and dragging me off toward his new garden behind Dad's house. "I do this while my white son sleeps," he explains, pointing to spaces reserved for red peppers, tomatoes, and beans. I'm astonished to see how he has succeeded in hacking his way through the brambles and bushes. Geoff tells me he goes out to this abandoned raspberry patch every afternoon and clears the brush, barefoot. He can't even feel the thorns. The gardening is better than shooting "bush meat," which was his original plan.

"How would be the taste of the squirrel or the raccoon?" he'd asked with a glint of hope in his eyes the day we met. "I would like to skin them and cook them." Jesus. What the fuck will the neighbors think? I'd wondered, catching a glimpse of animal carcasses skinned and hanging from tree branches. Last winter, neighbors were slowing down, "rubbernecking," Mom said, at the sight of the salt lick Dad had carted out on the lawn to attract deer. This in a county where ticks and Lyme disease are considered the seventh plague.

Uncle Larry suggested they skip the bush meat and shoot the Canadian geese down at our pond instead. "They don't migrate anymore," he said. "So I bet the flesh is a lot more tender. Not as tough as back when they flew south." The brief eruption of gunfire that followed scared the living bejesus out of the guy across the street. He called the cops. I don't really blame him. Nobody who moves to Connecticut's number one town expects to end up crawling around the floor of their living room, reenacting a scene from *Boyz N the Hood* or *New Jack City.*

It's nearly dark by the time Gordon and I finish our tour. Richard has hauled out a battered two-legged barbecue from the garage. I can hear the sounds of scraping as he attacks the rust with a wire brush. Bats streak in and out of the barn, and the sky is washed with brilliant bands of magenta, pink, and orange. I've forgotten how peaceful it can be with no one but my parents here — with Larry gone, Stan at work, and Geoff, recently reincarnated as a manager for a rock-and-roll band, somewhere on the road in upstate New York. *Thank God for Gordon,* I think to myself. *For this man who never fails to bring me down to earth.*

Although it has only been a bit more than eight weeks, it feels as if it were years ago, the day he popped into my father's house like the Coke bottle that fell out of the sky in *The Gods Must Be Crazy.* (A friend had dropped him off somewhere down the street.) With Dad due back by ambulance from his umpteenth hospital stay, the back house was full of those who come to make dying easier and cheaper for insurance companies: visiting nurses, grief counselors, guys delivering oxygen tanks the size of hot-water boilers.

There was Mother with her feet up on the couch. Wringing her hands and trying not to stare at this very large black man hovering behind her, she was telling everyone about the time she tried to strap a portable oxygen tank onto Dad's back like some deep-sea diver from *Jacques Cousteau.* "How was I supposed to know you dragged it in a cart behind you?" Only Gordon wasn't laughing. "So where, where did you say you were from?" came her querulous voice, at last.

"Aff-rica" was the one-word reply. Gordon's voice is deeper than Lake Victoria.

Mother's knowledge of "Aff-rica" is fairly limited: Tarzan (the books, not the movie), the uprising of the Mau Mau, *Hatari!*, and *King Solomon's Mines.* When he pulled out a plastic bag of green bananas, it was over. I could hear her silent moan of terror. As Geoff gently but firmly escorted her off the premises, she "shared" a few last words with the registered nurse.

"Would you please remove those roses this minute. You

know what happens to sick people in rooms with flowers? I'll tell you what happens. They die. That's right. D-E-A-D." Oh, Christ. At this point, Gordon, the nurse, the oxygen suppliers, they're bug-eyed. Maybe they figure Mom's anxious for all the obvious reasons. If only they knew the real reason. She has never allowed flowers in her own house for fear they would suck up all the — oxygen.

I needed to reassure Gordon. I also wanted to discreetly warn him about his patient — about Dad's swearing and the fact that he sometimes says things he doesn't mean, like "Jew. Jew." This is how he addressed my husband in the early days of his illness. "I am a stubborn prick" is his newest favorite. When my five-year-old daughter gave him a hug through his mask and he blurted that one out, she turned to me and said: "What's *stubborn* mean, Mom?"

We knew Dad would be a little shocked seeing Gordon, especially when he was expecting a nice white nurse with large breasts. "He's going to call him nigger. I know it," whispered my brother. "Tell him it's Tourette's, a tic or something. . . ."

It isn't his fault. It's aphasia. It's also bigotry, pure and simple. I like to think there's a kind of nobility in the savagery, in the excruciating honesty of both my parents' "conditions." But even as a native of these parts unknown, I have moments when I lose my bearings. When my sense of humor and of the absurd gives way to keening ululations, like those mourning Arab women in the movie *Foreign Legion,* I burrow my head beneath my pillows to stifle the sobs, and I pray to God the genes haven't found me.

Is this how I am going to die? I ask myself each and every time I get in the car and go back to New York. Am I going to die like my mother, so self-consumed, so whittled away by fear, I seem to just shrink and disappear? Or will I have a stroke at fifty-one like my father and leave my children to take care of a parent who has lost the power to move, to speak, and, most important, to comfort them? What if fear, rage, arrogance, and despair, like my genetic predispositions for alcoholism, osteoporosis, strokes, and cancer, are hardwired into my brain? What if I have already passed them on to my own children?

I wonder now if this is what all my words and the months of stiff-necked, nauseating loneliness at my keyboard are all about. A futile, desperate attempt to change what is "written," to fiddle with fate. Sometimes, I think this act of writing is all that's left of my innocence. In daring to put this story and these fears into words, perhaps I am somehow depriving them of their power to hurt or to harm me.

Other times, I can hear my mother yelling at the top of her voice: "I hate, I loathe, tattletales. Do you hear me?" And then I am gripped by the old terror of telling. Maybe these words are nothing more than a metaphor for my own aimlessness. Meandering everywhere but going nowhere, they're meaningless to all but those familiar with my own territory.

There are mornings in New York after the kids have gone to school when I go out to sit on the corner of 11th Street and sip a cappuccino. Slurping the foam from the hole in the lid of my cup, I find myself studying older people on the street with complete fascination and awe. I watch them accomplish ordinary, everyday acts like parallel parking, not to mention walking. "How do they do that?" I hear myself asking. Neither of my parents has parked a car or walked without help in years.

Ultimately, though, in this world of theme-parked travelers, a world in which one's own internal wilderness may soon go the way of the rain forest, its monsters tamed by doctors and drugs, my backyard is beginning to seem as mythically mysterious to me as the farthest corners of the earth. It is the last frontier, the place I have left the least explored. There are no maps. And memory is the only guide. But memory plays sneaky tricks on the unwary explorer. It leads down paths that seem as clearly marked as an alpine ski slope only to abandon one, skittering at the edge of yet another icy precipice. The precipice, unfortunately, is precisely where most of my family can usually be found. The edge is what keeps us on our toes.

"you're nothing but a depraved sadist!"

It couldn't be coincidence — that Mother's most terrible fear right now is of falling not just off her walker or out of her bed but over the edge of the precipice and into the abyss. "What if everyone thinks I'm dead and I'm not? What if they bury me breathing?" She's just posed this question to her lawyer, Nanette. The lawyer's pen seems to skip in slow motion across the conference table before it drops to the floor. As she ducks out of sight to retrieve it, I know she is also scrambling around under the table, attempting to retrieve whatever is left of her wits. "That only happens in fiction, Mary," the lawyer says ever so coolly, pushing a loose strand of hair into place.

Geoff and I are here at the lawyer's office with Mom to talk about her will. Her fears of death, for once, are far from unfounded. Her bones are so fragile that even a minor fall would splinter them into fragments as tiny and sharp as the Pick-Up

Sticks we played with when we were kids. We're trying to teach her to let go — to slide down like a drunk and gently hit the floor if she feels light-headed or dizzy. But for a woman who has relied on resistance all her life as her only means of control, relaxing isn't easy.

The jittery hands, the hobbling, the hump. It's so humiliating, it has her in tears. "Charles Laughton. That's who I look like. Charles Laughton as Quasimodo," she cries. "But maybe other people don't really notice," she adds. "What do you think?"

"Of course they don't notice." I lie, knowing perfectly well that people on the street slow down and stare at my mother as if she were the scene of some gruesome accident. They always have. She just never noticed. Before the hump, it was the one huge hoop earring, the curlers, the beads. There was nothing about my mother that offered other people even the remotest glimpse of themselves, nothing they recognized as familiar. As a kid, even her English sounded like Finnish.

"Come on, Jimmy. You can do it. Spell lu-bri-cious for me."

Jimmy was eight. Transfixed by the vision of so much female flesh peeking out at him from the holes in Mom's bra and underpants, Jimmy just stood there, stumped, while Mom went ahead with her gardening and sounded it out for him.

"Now ordinarily I'd tell you to look that word up in the dictionary. Use it in a sentence. But today I'm going to make it easy for you. It means unc-tuous."

"Yeah. Right, Mrs. Cullerton," said Jimmy, trying to tear his eyes away from her breasts.

"As in *smarmy. Oily.*"

"Uh-huh."

Mom liked to confound adults with her big words too. "So,

'ow was your din-hair zis evening, madame?" Pierre the Parisian headwaiter at Le Château, a local restaurant, would ask. "It was positively Lucullan, Pierre. Sa-lu-brious." Sa-what? *Pauvre* Pierre would fidget around as helplessly as Jimmy did, until I jumped in to translate. "She means it was delicious, really good, Pierre. Thank you."

Mom was like Yertle the Turtle, the way she piled up these words. The more syllables, synonyms, and adjectives she could fit into a sentence the better. She collected words. She acquired them as passionately, as compulsively, as other people acquire objects or possessions. They defined her. She scribbled them on the backs of envelopes, on torn-out blank pages from her books, on calendars. Once, I even found them sprinkled throughout her shopping list: *milk, eggs, juice, satrap, shibboleth, usufruct.* But Mom's facility with language, her gigantic vocabulary, had little to do with communicating. She used language as a form of one-upmanship, a competition or test that everyone but she and my father was destined to fail. Although she was an enormous presence in our lives, it was impossible to relate to her as a parent. And I hated her for it. I hated her not just for being different but for being indifferent: for not caring what I or anybody else thought. This is what made such foreigners of us all.

It wasn't just her vocabulary and the "Victrola." It wasn't the "icebox" or the black rotary telephone, which she still refuses to part with. Back in the sixties, everyone else had push-button Trimlines and Princesses, which Mother claimed were for "arrivistes." We couldn't even drive a normal car. A nice wood-paneled Ford station wagon like the Hills and the Simpsons. We had a gun-gray German-made Borgward. Who the hell ever heard of a Borgward? Except maybe for Joseph Goebbels and her dearest friend, Quirneken.

In those early Borgward years before I went away to boarding school, Dad was already commuting back and forth to Europe for Clarks. But while he made halfhearted attempts between flights to fit in — fixing things and furnishing the house with finds he'd unearthed in auctions — Mother talked ominously about "filthy lucre" and "affectation," about "climbers" and "phonies." "A house is for living in, not showing off," she'd say as I climbed on top of the couches, which I used as horses until the springs collapsed beneath the weight of my fantasies of becoming an equestrian.

Mom possessed an almost batlike sensitivity when it came to detecting the scent of a "climber" or a phony. It wasn't people like the DiMarcos up the street, with their gold-plated swan faucets and "Louis Louis" dining-room sets. "They're not vulgar," she'd say. "They're authentic." It wasn't people like the Lodges (I later went to school with one of Henry Cabot's granddaughters) or the writer Louis Auchincloss (I baby-sat for his family one summer). She was in awe of these people and their history. This made them equally genuine. No different, in that sense, from our baby-sitter, Mrs. Duryea. "A swamp Yankee" whom, despite living in a trailer and having a foul mouth, Mother respected for her "roots."

It was the discreet and cautious "Great Pretenders" in between. It was people who used euphemisms like *gift* (for *present*), *toilet tissue* (for *john paper*), *home* (for *house*), *wealthy* (for *filthy rich*), and *passed on, over,* or *away* (for *"plain old dead."*) It was women like the mother of a friend of my brother's at day school. Teeny Thorpe was a self-proclaimed "artist," "an eccentric." Everyone loved her. "She's the worst kind of conformist," Mom announced after picking Geoffrey up one afternoon. "She's the kind who pretends she isn't." In retrospect, Mom was right. There wasn't a single thing about Teeny or her lovely "home" and "atelier" that didn't shriek: "Look at me! Look at me! I'm an *artiste!*" (Mother always added the *e* when she talked about Teeny.)

When I was nine years old, Mother's batlike radar was totally wasted on me. What did I care if Teeny Thorpe was a "sham, an ostentatious bore"? So what if, as Mom pointed out on the way home, "there wasn't a single book in that entire house. I mean, it's incredible. Not one book." At least the button to Teeny's doorbell had never hung out from the wall on ten feet of bare wire. And her family owned a stereo, not a Victrola. She didn't pick her son up at school looking like some crazed Indian squaw, wearing stripes of chocolate-colored war paint and vicious purple lipstick. (Mother slathered on these incredibly thick streaks of Countess Isserlyn foundation blind, with no mirror. The streaks ended up covering the T zone only.) Teeny wore the barest hint of pink lipstick and a beat-up old straw hat that she'd picked up on a summer painting trip through Tuscany.

The idea of putting on a facade or caring about appearances was almost as hilarious to Mother as the idea of Teeny, or anybody else for that matter, in Tuscany. For Mother, appearances weren't just deceiving. They were meaningless. They were the side effects of envy. For Mother, envy was a form of ignorance. This was one of her saving graces. She was a compulsive liar, but she told nothing but the truth (as she saw it) about what made a human being. It didn't matter if you were the president, the pope, or the neighbor down the street.

On the November morning in 1963 when Kennedy was

shot, the two of us were doing errands at Woolworth. Shoppers were falling to their knees all around us in the aisles. They were crying while Mother went on casually flinging toilet paper, toothbrushes, and cold cream into her basket. "Mom, didn't you hear that? It's the president." "Mmmmm," she said. After piling the bags into the car and sliding into the driver's seat, she looked me straight in the eye and said, "It's awful. No one should have to die like that. But that man's father was nothing but a philandering Irish bootlegger."

Squirming in my seat, I was picturing what would happen if anyone heard her. We'd be stoned to death in the parking lot like the woman in Shirley Jackson's story "The Lottery." "He bought his feckless son into the White House."

"OK, Mom. OK." I sighed, rolling up my window. "He wasn't a hero," she added before stripping the gears as if for emphasis. "He cheated his way through Harvard just like his brother did."

So much for Camelot. When I returned to the convent and Mother Brady sat us all down in her classroom to discuss the tragedy, the echo of Mom's words was ricocheting around so loudly in my head, I was sure I was about to be sent off to the headmistress's office. I'd have to walk around at recess wearing a sandwich board. DAUGHTER OF A TRAITOR it would say in bold black letters.

Mom wasn't a traitor. She believed it was "character," not money or fame, that made the man. Celebrities bored her almost as much as the Brownies, the PTA, and Teeny Thorpe. It was the ability and the courage to think — it was "the life of the mind" — she valued most. In the end, Mom may have been afraid to get out of her car, but she was never afraid to ask a question. She was pathetically inept when it came to small talk. But get her going on the big stuff — on her books or the movies of Godard, Rossellini, and Joseph Losey — and she'd talk your ear off.

Unfortunately, these weren't exactly hot topics up in our neck of the woods. A lot of the "brains" had to be imported from the city or abroad. "God! What a brain! That man has read everything," Mom said, blithely waving at this person, weaving away in his car in the distance. The man, Steven Hadley, was a brain. But he'd completely lost his mind. The son of a New York tugboat titan, a chain-smoker, and a heavy drinker, he'd just spent two days at our summerhouse on Lake Candlewood ducking behind couches and yelling, "The CIA is coming! The CIA is coming!" While Dad coaxed Steven out from his hiding place under piles of coats in the hall closet, Mom pooh-poohed his paranoid schizophrenia as "a case of frayed nerves." "He's highly strung," she said. "It can happen to anyone."

Compared to Steven, Mom's own nerves seemed no more frayed than the plastic threads hanging from the hem of her double-knit polyester pants. I didn't dislike him or any of Mother's other weird and unusual friends. But I did wonder why our dog, Pal, seemed to be even more highly strung than they were. I remember when he bit the eye out of Flip, the DiMarcos' miniature French poodle. "Dogs are dogs," Mom explained to the infuriated, grieving family in a scene that would foreshadow her later encounter with the mailman. "It's perfectly natural — the instinct to attack." Every afternoon, we jumped off the school bus and saw that furry hole in Flip's face; we felt awful.

The instinct to attack. This was the trait Pal and Mother shared and that made them so inseparable. Pal wasn't a pet. He was Mom with paws — a husky that had leaped with a snarl and gnashing of teeth right from the pages of one of her Jack London novels into her lap. He was her Buck, her White Fang — a daily reminder of the call and tug of the wild and of the war Mother waged against the world each and every day of her life.

Pal took the same liberties with the law that Mom did. The two of them were in total cahoots against the powers that be. "Sadist. You're nothing but a depraved sadist!" she'd scream at the dog warden when he threatened to throw Pal in the pound. Yet again. "Who do you think you are? Telling me my dog needs a license?"

Pal had every right to gallivant around the neighborhood, scavenging through garbage cans, chasing cars, lunging for the eyeballs of tiny poodles, and "deflowering bitches in heat." Mom seemed to caress every syllable of that phrase, almost as if she took pleasure in Pal's reputation as a rogue male.

Among the many bitches Pal deflowered were two German shepherds owned by a Mr. Von Wellsheim. Mr. Von Wellsheim was an Austrian. "Too Teutonic," Mom would say when she saw him, strutting about in his knife-creased jodhpurs and knee-high black leather boots. He even carried a crop. But horses and dogs were his pride and joy. When Pal, our Poky Little Puppy, tunneled his way into the kennel and screwed his prize shepherds, it broke his heart.

"Breeding dogs is my business, Mary. People pay me for purebreds, for pedigree. What am I going to do?"

"I'm so sorry, Andre," Mom said, on the verge of giggling, "but you can't blame Pal. It was a full moon."

"Pedigree. Purebreds. My foot!" she harrumphed after slamming down the phone. "His roots are showing, that's all." (The roots were a reference to Austrian Nazis, not Mr. Von Wellsheim's hair.)

Mother called Nazis, *Naah-hzis.* The way she talked about war, you'd've thought she just caught a piece of shrapnel in her leg or got gassed at the front: the Boer War, the Great War, WWII (referred to by letters and the number only), Teddy's storming of San Juan Hill. Mom took war and history personally. She lived every day as if it were yesterday. Thanks to her "elephantine memory," there wasn't a December 7 that went by, even when we grew up, without a message from her on our answering machines about "the Nips" and Pearl Harbor: "Just thought you'd like to know. Today was the day of infamy." *Beep.* When Mom saw a Toyota on Main Street (this was when they first started importing Japanese cars), she'd make that whistling sound like a bomb dropping. "How dare people forget what they did to us?" she'd mutter furiously.

Conflict made Mother feel alive. If there didn't happen to be a real war going on, she created one. As she battled her way along Main Street, we would duck for cover when we saw her striding out of stores and slamming doors: "Ingrate! Filthy cur! I will never go into that bank [market, post office, deli, diner] again." She provoked people constantly. Her own day of infamy, famous in family folklore, was the day my father accompanied her to court in Danbury, where she planned to argue a fine for speeding. "Just pay up, Mary, and for Christ's sake," he implored her, "try and be quiet!" But Mother couldn't resist. Twisting her handkerchief (she was never without a handkerchief. She kept it balled up and stuffed in her sleeve), she approached the bench.

"Your Highness?" she called up to the judge as my father blanched and the courtroom guffawed. "Excuse me, I mean Your Excellency, milord." It wasn't on purpose. She was so nervous, she forgot how to address him. The judge was apoplectic. He doubled her fine and had her expelled from the premises.

Mother's resistance to the powers that be never let up, not even when she moved beyond the boundaries of her own backyard and encountered forces more intractable than her own. Most memorable of all these encounters for me was her border incident with Canadian immigration. This took place eight months after my Parisian homecoming and en route to Montreal, where I had become a student at McGill.

Much to Dad's chagrin, I had chosen McGill over his alma mater, Dartmouth, in the hope I could keep up with my French. (Futile as it turned out. The Quebecois didn't understand a single thing I said — not in French or in English.) My fondest memories of the whole experience are of the months I spent eating huge gobs of chocolate icing off the tops of frozen Sara Lee cakes and the train trips to and from Stamford, Connecticut. Passing through the landscape of ice and snow, shimmering like a quilt of silver and sequins at dawn, I felt like Lara in *Dr. Zhivago*.

Unlike Dad, Mother was delighted with my choice. "I've always wanted to go to Ottawa. If I had to choose one city in all the world to see, it would be Ottawa."

"McGill isn't *in* Ottawa, Mom. It isn't even near frigging Ottawa."

"Well, it's in Canada, isn't it? I'm mad about Canada."

This was true. Much like her undying love for the Jewish

people, a love based almost entirely on her girlhood friendship with Rita Feinson, Mother's infatuation with Canada was based on the fact it was the home of singer Gordon Lightfoot. It was where writers Mordecai Richler, Robertson Davies, and Hugh MacLennan were born.

Mom loved riding the train most of all, however. Which is why she decided to join me on my trip up to Canada at the end of August, and why we were waiting at Stamford Station together. Bob, a very polite seventeen-year-old English houseguest and the son of a friend of my father's at Clarks, had been cajoled into acting as her chauffeur.

One of the many European "refugees" who came to live at my parents' house in the summertime, Bob had been packing shoes at Dad's warehouse in Norwalk. He planned to use the money he'd earned to take off and see a bit of America before flying home to England. Unbeknownst to Bob, Mother had decided that he would see a bit of Canada first.

"Mary, I'd love to keep you company on the train, but look at me." Bob was pointing to his bare chest, bathing suit, and sandals.

"C'mon, Bob. It'll be an adventure, great fun."

"But, Mary, I can't. I didn't bring anything with me, not even my passport. They won't let me across the border."

"Oh, don't be an ass, Bob. Of course they will. I'll talk to them. They'll understand."

The only one surprised when they didn't understand was Mother. "This is ludicrous, do you hear me? Absurd!" she whined to the uniform who was escorting Bob off the train. "Listen, lady. You're entering another country here. Nobody goes across without a passport. Nobody." For Mother, international borders were an insignificant detail. Good Godfrey! She was leaving me at the station and turning right around and coming home. We waved to Bob as he stood there on the platform in his bathing suit and sandals. He'd borrowed a shirt from me, and Mother had loaned him thirty dollars for the bus ride home.

"Petty people with a little power" is how Mother summed up the incident at the border. But unlike her bumper-sticker heroes — Chavez, Bobby Sands, the Indians, and Ralph Nader — Mom only pretended to be a rebel. Her fear of real authority figures like her father and her husband was surpassed only by her fear of everything else: elevators, fire, flying, flowers, bats, birds, rats, thunderstorms, trains, death, New York. Sometimes, I think that's the reason she wore so much perfume — to mask the smell of those fears. But not even the overwhelmingly pungent aroma of Joy was strong enough to fool us.

Mom was her own worst enemy. But confronting these imaginary rivals gave her something to talk about over her six-o'clock jigger of bourbon, orange juice, and bitters. It was an act of exorcism that gave her an illusion of power and a fleeting glimpse of the "somebody" she might have been.

The thing is, Mom was more than just a somebody. She was a one-woman show. There were no gray areas in her life. Unlike other women who were obliged to scale down the dimensions of their lives and create a world small enough to manage as mothers and housewives, Mom wasn't interested in managing. Or in being a mother or a housewife. Her dream was to be the editor in chief of a big-city newspaper. Even the word *managing* repelled her. It suggested the drab dreariness of Mr. Gradgrind in *Hard Times,* with his pitiless request for facts, nothing but the facts. "Facts bore the pants off me," she used to say.

"The poor woman is disturbed," a friend's mother once whispered to her husband out near their garage, where her daughter and I were rehearsing a scene from *The Wizard of Oz.* (I had definitely inherited Mother's theatrical flair, along with her ability to improvise and invent.) Sure, my mother was disturbed. But unlike my friend's mother and other mothers like her, Mom couldn't stand being dull or dulled. She found no comfort in conventional distractions like heavy drinking, decorating, shopping, or drugs. Mom wouldn't even take Novocain at the dentist in those days. "A little pain never hurt anyone," she'd say with a chuckle before dropping us off to get cavities filled at Dr. Silver's.

But witnessing my mother's public performances — the acting out of private fears, rage, and unhappiness — made me so excruciatingly self-conscious as a child and so uncomfortable in my own skin that I dreamed only of being someone else. Disguise came as naturally to me as a ten-year-old playing the Wicked Witch in a neighborhood garage as it did later in life. Much later. When I told friends I felt like a different person when I traveled on ships and trains, I really meant it. I was a different person.

In 1978, I traveled on Amtrak as a French girl named Brigitte all the way from California to New York. I was returning from a week shooting toy commercials in LA. My fear of flying was so extreme in those days, I had even talked my creative director into letting me take the train to Cincinnati for client presentations. I don't know what possessed me that particular Sunday morning as I laid out my nightgown and champagne picnic in my roomette. I just remember seeing an absolutely stunning older man walking down the platform. He told me his name was Gardner McKay. He'd sailed around the world for years in a TV show called *Adventures in Paradise.* I was as shocked as he was when I opened my mouth and began speaking English with a French accent so thick, he had to strain and squint to understand me.

Gardner was smitten. My diesel-driven fantasies lasted across the Rockies through Chicago, Washington, and over the Hudson. And then I made a fatal mistake. Instead of kissing him good-bye at Penn Station, I lent him my parents' apartment. I still have to give my father credit. When he returned to New York early from Europe and found this stranger wandering around his living room, raving about the charms of a girl named Brigitte, he didn't bat an eye. He put his bags down, closed the bedroom door, and phoned me. "Brigitte?" He chuckled while I spluttered and choked. "Don't even try and explain. I'm going out to dinner. Kindly have your friend out of here by the time I come back."

There was also the summer I worked at the Scottish Bakehouse in Martha's Vineyard and served scones and sausage patties with a burr so thick, customers would run out to their cars and drag people in just to hear my funny accent. I pretended I was the owner's niece "cuum" over from Edinburgh "fur a bi' a the suun and sea." I tied up their "wee bits of shortbread" and rattled on about the "Firth a Forth" right up to the final day of reckoning, when the owner, Mrs. White (who was a true Scot), popped out of the kitchen and said she'd heard just about enough about her nonexistent niece and would I please stop the playacting and get back to work.

"Liar, liar. Pants on fire!" Mom would have said. I suppose it was another form of flight. But the playacting, my traveling incognito, was also about keeping a low profile while trying to locate the stranger within. So what if there seemed to be as many strangers in there as some schizophrenic Sybil? As Mother had taught me, life was a stage — a real stage, with no metaphor intended — and everyone on it but us was an extra.

"only the nouveaux swim in pools."

NEITHER MATURITY NOR MIDDLE AGE SEEMS TO HAVE exactly cured me of this childish need to pretend I'm someone I'm not. For the past five years, I've been reserving my favorite table at Il Cantinori, an Italian restaurant near our loft in the West Village, under the name Davis. Even the best friends who come in to join me for dinner on Tuesday nights know enough to ask for the Davis party. After all this time, I imagine that Frank, the maître d', must be a bit perplexed, especially when I insist on paying the bill with a credit card that says Brenda Cullerton. I mean, why this need to keep a low profile and to use an alias when no one knows who the hell I am, anyway? Who am I hiding from?

And it gets worse, this game of make-believe. Two weeks ago, at the end of March, I was regaling my Israeli periodontist with tales of being a war correspondent. For weeks, every time this macho bald-headed guy cut my gums open, I pictured him running up and down the Golan Heights with an Uzi. For some reason, I figured maybe he'd empathize enough with my own stories of being four-months pregnant during the Romanian revolution, hitching a ride in a tank, and crawling away on my swollen belly through a hail of gunfire on the streets of Bucharest to give me a discount. Which he did. He took four hundred bucks off the bill.

It sounds crazy, using an alias at a favorite restaurant and telling tales like this at forty-seven years old to one's periodontist. But if that fantasy of being a war correspondent had taken place in a dream and not in his office, it wouldn't have been crazy at all. This is the thing about coming from a place where there are no metaphors. The subconscious ceases to exist, and everything from fears to dreams becomes real.

It isn't the hope of a discount that has me recounting my imaginary war stories to Dr. Prywes. It's revisiting and reliving memories of a childhood spent in the trenches with a woman devoted to conflict. It's these trips to Ridgefield. This is what this fantasy of risking my life in Romania for the sake of a good story is about. It's about the reality of me telling this story about my family and the fears of what will become of me once it is finished.

It wasn't easy, keeping a low profile when I was a child. Not when everything Mother did either pulled us into the spotlight or put us in the line of friendly fire. The Flip incident, when Pal ripped the eyeball off the face of the DiMarcos' dog, marked the end of our invitations to swim in their aboveground swimming pool.

"Pools are obscene. They're disgusting!" Mom ranted. "Only the nouveaux swim in pools."

Nouveau. That was it — the kiss of death. As kids, we had no problems with the idea of a pool, especially on muggy, hot days when the Norwalk River dried up and defied our contorted efforts to wriggle around and get wet. The sound of splashing up the hill was torture.

Mr. DiMarco was a hairdresser who drove around in a Caddy with a trunk full of cash. My parents thought he was a low-level mobster. His wife, Beth, hardly ever left the house. A heavily dyed redhead, she padded around the kitchen in dirty white slippers and a bathrobe and spent most of the daylight hours sipping from a heavy cut-crystal glass full of Scotch and melted ice cubes.

Beth was so brittle, you could see the cracks through the layers of powder on her face. She also had the world's tiniest sneeze. My mother had the loudest. "Don't ever suppress a sneeze," she used to advise us, while looking up at the sun and working herself into a sonic boom that was almost as deafening as the blowing that came after.

Beth's appearances in the "breezeway" were our cue for a Kool-Aid break. Kool-Aid and being allowed into the house were special treats. I loved touching the wallpaper. It had raised red velour fleur-de-lis all over it, just like I'd seen at Tad's Steak House in New York after the Madison Square Garden Horse Show. There were marble sinks in the bathrooms, lots of gilded and glass furniture, and white shag carpets.

Even more unbelievable, every kid had his or her own television. Of course, we had no television. Mom was one of the very few who knew for a fact that there were rays inside every TV that were killing people. But there was something inanimate about the DiMarco house. Shrouded and reeking of stale cigarette smoke, it was spooky but spiritless.

The DiMarcos' son, Tommy, was the neighborhood bully. One afternoon, he talked a bunch of us younger girls into going up to his clubhouse on the mountain. I was eight years old. Somehow, he also talked a few of us into lying down on the rocks and pulling down our pants so he and his friends could stick a three-inch nail up our vaginas and see if we were sick.

If the nail had red on it, it was a bad sign. I can still feel the shock of cold air and metal as he pushed it in. "Tell your parents and you'll die," was all he said when we got up and ran. I don't know if the boys were ever punished. Tommy was dead at twenty-five, murdered in a drug hit in Dallas. Whatever was left of the child in me was aborted with that nail. In keeping the horror of it a secret from my mother, I was trying to protect her. I'd heard people laugh and make fun of her. She was the one who seemed defenseless and ridiculous, not me. By protecting her, I was inflating my own sense of power.

It wasn't until 1979, twenty years later, while watching a doctor hammer a two-inch steel pin into a woman's hip with no anesthetic, that the memory of that moment on the mountain finally surfaced. I was in a hospital in the north of China, a country I had once imagined I could reach by digging through the dirt and roots in my own backyard with a kitchen spoon. A group of us traveling on the *QE2* had been invited to observe acupuncture surgery at a local hospital in the town of Dalian.

I had taken a "sabbatical" from Grey Advertising at the time and had booked myself a ten-day passage on the *QE2* from Hong Kong to Yokohama, Japan, where I planned to hop a train up north to Nagata and then an Aeroflot flight into Siberia. I still remember the guffaws of my creative director, Sam Abelow, when I asked for a "sabbatical."

"This is an ad agency, Brenda, not graduate school. We don't give sabbaticals."

"C'mon, Sam. Please . . ."

"Look, Brenda, do you know anyone else in this office who is allowed to take the f'ing train to and from California for shoots? Who pops across Chicago in a taxi to get her hair done at Marshall Field's while the rest of us are back here finishing storyboards? The answer is no!"

"But I want to write a book, Sam," I pleaded. "I even have the title."

"Aha," he said, sitting up a bit straighter in his chair. "What's the title?"

"'Vagabondage.'"

I'd been in advertising long enough by then to know that almost every creative director dreamed of writing a book. But it was the title that sold him. The last words I ever heard from Sam came as he flipped through another storyboard and waved good-bye to me from his door. "The closest most people will ever come to your slow boats to China is a long weekend at Great Gorge," he said. "Have a wonderful trip." (Great Gorge, a Playboy resort in the Catskills, was one of my accounts.) Sam died of a heart attack one month later, while backing his VW out of the Westport Train Station.

Winters in my midtwenties when I was living in New York were the toughest time of year for me. Gray, in every sense of the word. While friends happily hibernated with boyfriends, I longed only to be gone. These friends were native

New Yorkers who had lived their whole lives in the city. They had serious jobs and a future. They seemed to know exactly where they were going. I had landed in New York after eight years in boarding schools, two years in Europe, and another year in Montreal. Whatever money I earned in advertising went to pay for summer trips on ocean liners and airplanes. Few of my friends understood this irrepressible need of mine to move on. When I tried to explain how I felt at the start of a journey, that glorious moment when feelings suddenly stir from a standstill and take off, they just shrugged. For me, flight time meant another limbo left behind.

This trip to China, the first not just for me but for the *QE2*, had also included brief bus excursions to Guangzhou and Beijing before the sail up the coast to Dalian. Not far from the old Port Arthur and the Russian border, Dalian was as cold as the Manchu, towering giants who stopped and stared and whose grimaces froze my grins into place. There was something sinister, ominous, about the city. Not even the sun seemed to give much warmth. The city's nerves were as on edge as my own. China had invaded Vietnam, and the possibility of war with Russia didn't seem far-fetched.

I shivered when I heard that the mountains surrounding the city and along the border were hollow, that iron doors opened into a network of stone tunnels and caverns that snaked back into an underground city. Within thirty minutes of a warning siren, the town's entire population would disappear off the face of the earth.

But the hospital was a cheerier, more familiar place. Hovering above the operating theater in a glass bubble, I had no explanation for the sudden rush of intimacy I felt with this woman who had been wheeled in on a gurney beneath me. She was bathed in the greenish light of fluorescent bulbs and had hundreds of needles piercing her feet and spine. A nurse gently massaged her forehead while an electric current warmed the needles, turning them imperceptibly. The needles were shutting her nerve centers down. She was smiling.

Following the doctor's hand as he took hold of the scalpel and made his incision, I felt this tingling sensation in my thigh and reached down as if to close her gaping wound. I couldn't believe there was so little blood. Wincing while I waited for her screams of agony, I was told she was floating in a state of "mild discomfort." When the pin was placed in her hip and her body began to shake with the force of the doctor's blows, I collapsed. After the hole in her side was sewn together and the needles were removed, the woman was wrapped like an infant in miles of clean white cotton.

Maybe it was my own wish to be swaddled like an infant, or the sudden, inexplicable longing to be taken care of, that brought me back to that moment of helplessness with Tommy on the mountain. There was such relief in the release of the memory, I couldn't stop crying. For years, I had been floating around in a state of mild discomfort — feeling other people's pain so I wouldn't feel my own.

Could this be what my life as a sleeper, slipping in and out of other people's skins, was really all about? An attempt to see and experience life through their eyes, to speak their language, to feel not just with but for them? Only then would I become part of a world bigger than the tiny, tortured one that kept my mother at such odds with everyone but her dogs. But the process of assimilation was so complete, I had disappeared along the way. My own emotions had become weirdly dislocated.

"Is OK, my flend. OK," the guide whispered as I sat sobbing in a rickety old wooden chair that morning. Suddenly those moments when I had always felt most alive — sitting on trains or hurtling along runways, being propelled forever forward — gave way to a vacuum. I was tired of rekindling old flames in faraway places and of seeking shelter in the arms of strangers. As I gulped for air and longed for space, the guide whisked me off to Tiger Beach, an ocean park with paths paved in pink pebbles and shells. Patterns of stars and flowers unfolded like a tapestry beneath my feet.

Wandering along the twists and turns, I felt like Dorothy on the Yellow Brick Road. But unlike Dorothy, I was twenty-seven years old. I had slept in silk-canopied beds in some of Europe's grandest castles, camped in farmhouses, sailed across the oceans, and nestled into the bunks behind truck-drivers' cabs while slipping over the borders of England, Ireland, Spain, and Italy. I had met aristocrats, farmers, communists, and students. I spoke three foreign languages. But I had no home. Skittering along the edge of that path in China, I saw rocks and cliffs as sharp as tiger's teeth jutting out into the water as waves slapped up against the sand below. Only the fury of the sea seemed to calm me. Three women offered me a bite of the seaweed they'd carried up in baskets from the beach. It tasted of the salt of tears.

I hated the taste of tears. Even on that afternoon with Tommy so long ago, when the thrust of that nail had punctured whatever last-minute hopes I might have had of escape or rescue, there had been no tears, only terror. The terror of telling. Not telling made me brave. As brave as Pal, who ran off to lick his own wounds and die in the woods when he got hit chasing a car. "Leave him alone," Mom said when we volunteered to go and find him, to bring him home. "He's gone off to the happy hunting grounds," she explained. "He doesn't need a vet."

All of our dogs but Sandy — Pal, Fuss, Natty Bumpo — seemed to get hit by cars and die alone in the woods. (When Sandy, the dog that took a chunk out of the mailman's leg, was finally put to sleep, Mother told my kids he'd gone away on vacation to Florida.) If it had been only pets that Mother abandoned the moment they showed signs of weakness or mortality, I might have accepted her tales about the happy hunting grounds. But it was people too: her father when he got sick, my father when he had his stroke, her younger sister Brenda (the sister I was named after and who died of cancer at fifty-three), Great-auntie Rhodie, even her friend Josephine, who lived down the road. For the three years it took this woman who lived a short two-minute walk away to die, my mother visited precisely twice. They spoke on the phone for hours instead.

The phone has always been Mother's umbilical cord and remains one of the few connections to the outside world she hasn't yet severed. But like the wall that divides our house, it is also a symbol of her inability to communicate, her need for distance. Even physical contact embarrasses my mother. Her whole body still stiffens and shrinks when she's hugged or kissed. The phone is a means of staying in touch without being touched.

I remember a phone call I made to her years ago. I was

twenty-two and had a job in Florence selling jewelry to tourists on the Ponte Vecchio for the summer. I liked being invited up to the rooms above the shops where tiny gnarled men repaired broken clasps on golden necklaces and the delicate filigreed settings of precious rings that, like me that lonely summer, had lost their grip. It was an impulse that sent me to the train station to call home.

As I huddled in the booth, the connection was so bad that I had to shout through bursts of static.

"Pray for your brother and his friends," Mom said, her voice fading in and out over the wire.

"What do you mean, pray for him?" I screamed back, clutching the receiver.

"Two of his friends were killed in a car crash last night. He was in the front seat."

"Jesus, Mom. How badly is he hurt?"

"He's fine, dear. Just a few scratches."

"When are you going to see him?"

"I'm not. I'm tired. Your father and I are going golfing at Hilton Head."

I hung up on her. Three weeks later, there was a letter from my father in the mailbox. It was two sentences long:

Darling:
Please keep in mind that when you hang up on someone, you're not just cutting them off, you're cutting yourself off too.

Love, Dad

I never forgot those words of wisdom. But I never forgot the context in which they were written, either. When I flew down to California three months later to visit this brother I hardly knew, a brother I had left at home when I went to boarding school at eleven years old, Geoff told me that his friend's Alfa had slammed into a tree at fifty miles per hour. He'd crawled out the windshield and sat by the side of the road for twenty minutes, waiting for the ambulance while his friends bled to death in the car.

"So many losses," Mom now moans from her bed. "No one should have to bear so many losses." In listening to her repeat the names of those with whom she has battled or abandoned over the years, I think it's her penance, this endless litany of the lost. An act of contrition similar to the Hail Marys and Our Fathers I raced through while fingering the beads of a pink plastic rosary in the convent, where my life as a sleeper began.

"only lazy slobs sit on lawn mowers!"

THE CONVENT IN ALBANY WHERE I ARRIVED ON A SATurday afternoon with my green monogrammed trunk was also known as the Mother House. It was where postulants and novices trained to become full-fledged brides of Christ. Friends there always joked about my being an orphan. There was nothing in my rooms or in my conversations that alluded to family, and I often chose to stay behind when others went home on long weekends and holidays. Even my cubicle was as neat and spartan as the nuns' next door. But this castlelike building, complete with parapets and bell towers, was my salvation. Just as it had been for my mother before me. "My Reverend Mother was none other than Eleanor Barry herself," she told me the morning I was packing my trunk. "She was Phil Barry's daughter, the man who wrote *Philadelphia Story.*"

Unlike other girls, I even loved the uniform: a navy-blue-and-white-checked wool jumper, white blouse with Peter Pan collar, kneesocks, and saddle shoes. The minute I put the uniform on, I became invisible. I looked just like everybody else. To the daughter of a mother who gardened in black baggy underpants and who set off titters every time she walked down Main Street, this invisibility seemed miraculous.

Although the nuns at the convent disapproved of my close friendships with older girls, they were proud of the way I protected those who lived on the periphery of belonging. It wasn't just foreigners like my Caracas friend, Cecilia, and her clique of rich South American girls; it was girls like Theresa. Theresa was a real orphan, a black girl and a boarder from the Albany ghetto who slept in the cubicle next to mine. She was also an epileptic. When she went into convulsions, writhing on the bathroom floor, her mouth filled with foaming spit, other girls would stare, drop their toothbrushes, and run out screaming.

Together with the nun in charge, I would come in and lie down on the floor next to her, quietly talking and touching her hair until the seizure passed. It wasn't pity that had me keeping Theresa company on the floor. This was a girl who I imagined probably prayed every night for the power to become invisible but who lay helpless and exposed on a cold tile floor instead, with her nightgown halfway up her thighs. It was instinct that had me rushing in to comfort and to cover her. I felt the terror of her nakedness.

Within the secluded walls of the convent, I also discovered that there was a rhythm to life, a certain pace that made tricks like leaping out of moving cars in church parking lots totally unnecessary. It was a rhythm that relied on the sound of bells. The chapel bells, our signal to kneel, sit, and stand, were silver. They tinkled like the one my grandmother shook at the dining-room table when the buzzer under the carpet was broken. The bells in the dormitories and classrooms were heavier. Made of brass with wooden handles, they marked the time for everything from eating and sleeping to study hall and recreation.

The bells, the rules, and the monthly ritual of awarding blue or green ribbons for good behavior helped anchor me. They established boundaries that until then I had conjured up on my own, like Harold with his purple crayon, by drawing imaginary lines everywhere, including down the middle of the bedroom I shared with my sister at home. I charged her a nickel every time she crossed it. Perhaps that imaginary line was a strange foreshadowing of the wall my mother would later build between herself and my father.

But here at the convent, the lines were drawn for me. I felt safe with Mother Tighe, Mother Cotter, and Reverend Mother Fitzgerald. With the swish of their long black skirts and their lace-up leather pumps, they hardly seemed to touch the ground. Their vanishing acts behind dorm curtains and cloister doors gave even their inaccessibility an irresistible allure.

This allure of the inaccessible that began with a longing to explore the mysterious world that lay just beyond those cloister doors may well have been born from textbook longings for the love and affection of distant parents. But I'm grateful for it. Without it, I never would have journeyed to hospital rooms in China or to Tahitian atolls or to those equally remote, unreachable regions that lay hidden deep within the depths of other human beings. I have always been attracted to the darkness of these depths, to the void that lies beneath facade. The more closely guarded and inaccessible that region, the more determined I have always been to conquer it.

Because it is there within that void, where others are the most fearful, that I have always felt the most at home and the least afraid. Maybe this is also why I prefer to live in other people's skins and have chosen to become a protector, a confidante, and a confessor. Not just because it shields me or allows me to discreetly disappear within other people's dramas and dreams. But because I have been given the power to console. And in consoling, I am consoled.

Yet when I see my mother now, this woman who, for me, has always been the most inaccessible and inconsolable of all, this woman I call *Ma, Mom,* and the more formal *Mother,* but never *Mommy* (*Mommy,* with all its implications of dependence, just doesn't fit this still-distant figure on the bed), I feel so far away, I don't know what to say.

Geoff insists on taking her back to the doctors for tests. But they still can't find anything wrong — no cancer or blood disease, no tumors, nothing that explains such disorientation or fatigue. An orthopedist finally fit her for a back brace. She says it looks like something from the Flying Wallendas.

Mother's been taking more than twenty vitamins a day for over thirty years. She's never even had a common cold or flu. Now she can barely dial her rotary phone. The Visiting Nurse Association is trying to talk us into moving her into some kind of assisted-living environment. If, by *assisted living,* they're referring to something along the lines of the queen of England with her court of ladies-in-waiting, Mother might just fit in. But one look at the brochures from the ConstaCare Corporation, with their harrowing promises of "a worry-free, engaging lifestyle, peace of mind, and people who really know how to have fun," pretty much annihilates all hopes for her. Fun has never been Mother's idea of a good time.

Euphemisms, acronyms, and smiles abound in the video for the Maples on Bethnal Green. Following in the camera's footsteps, I drift in through the marble hallway, with its grand staircase and Ethan Allened lobby, past the Wellness Center ("Arggh!" I can hear Mom saying) and the Evergreen Residence ("a locked but warm and cozy environment for those suffering from Alzheimer's and memory disorders"). The cloying voice of the narrator sounds as phony as the veneer of marble in the hallway as "we" head toward the Beauty Shop and the Activities Room. Here, I am asked to push Pause on my machine and check my ADL. "It's an insert," continues the voice from nowhere as I fumble through the masses of paper and glossy photos. "What the fuck is an ADL?" I mutter. "Ah. Right. The Activities of Daily Living sheet."

When the tour resumes, the narrator talks about how much "the community, the family, enjoys bird-watching, bingo, the Lawrence Welk and Richard Rodgers sing-alongs, and ice cream socials." Mother used to say Lawrence Welk looked like someone who'd been stuffed in a taxidermist's shop.

Who are these people all dressed up with nowhere to go but the grave? And how did they get here? When the camera stops and focuses on a collage a man is proudly pointing at outside his room, I push Eject and snatch the video out from the machine. "Tom" made the collage in Arts and Crafts with his crafts instructor, Delores. Inside this framed wooden box, he's glued photographs of the family that has deserted him: of his son and smiling grandchildren, his dead wife and dog.

I picture that man crying into his pillow at night, wondering how he ended up in this palace of the purposeless. The foundations are so shaky, the facade so flimsy, I think, just like Mother does, that these people should be stood up against a wall and shot. Not the "discerning seniors," not even the family members who put them there, but the merciless group of suits from the ConstaCare Corporation who have sentenced humans to death by watching endless reruns of Lawrence Welk.

I prefer to allow my mother to find her own way to the happy hunting grounds.

"Promise you won't ever put me in the hospital," she begs. "Please promise."

"I promise, Ma."

She's made a decision.

And I have no right to intervene. Other families might insist on taking their mother to a hospital, on hooking her up to an IV to force-feed her. For us, this would only postpone the inevitable. Because no one has ever succeeded in force-feeding my mother anything.

We have, however, finally hired another live-in helper. It's Gordon who introduced us. Her name is Bernice. Like Gordon, Bernice is from the Akan tribe in Ghana. Her real name is Abena. It means Tuesday. Everyone in Ghana is named after the day of the week on which he or she was born. Gordon is Friday. *Kofi.* He says Friday men are stronger and smarter than Wednesdays and Sundays.

Bernice has fourteen brothers and sisters. She's the second of her siblings to leave her village in the Volta River Delta for America, the land of opportunity. Of the $185 a day we pay her agency, she takes home $70. Considering how intimately this woman relates to my mother, listening to her daydreams and nightmares, combing her hair, and feeding her, my ignorance about her seems inexcusable. So I look up Ghana in my atlas.

Using my finger to trace its boundaries with Togo and the Ivory Coast, I move inland from the capital city of Accra, on the Bight of Benin, toward the Delta, passing towns with unpronounceable names like Koforidua, Akuse, and Mpraeso. It is as if in making this physical gesture, in putting my finger on the village where she was born, I will get to know her better.

Like Gordon, Bernice doesn't like wearing shoes. Perhaps she finds comfort in feeling the hard-packed ground beneath her feet. I imagine it reminds her of home — like the plantains, potatoes, and vegetables she brings with her from Brooklyn to eat. I have never met gentler, more graceful human beings than these "denizens of the dark continent," as Mother used to call them. They walk straight-backed and tall with pride. Unlike Mother, they are unbroken.

For them, Fairfield County, one of the richest, most privileged areas of America, must seem like the end of civilization. How else can they explain the absurdity, the obscenity, of a white woman slowly dying of malnutrition while her husband gorges himself to death on Hershey bars and peanut-butter-and-jelly sandwiches next door and of children who seem to abandon the care of their own flesh and blood to strangers?

The kitchen tables in both my parents' houses are piled with clipboards and "progress reports." "No Care to Be Given Unless Circled," it says on the top of the Home Health Aide Activity sheets. I usually avoid looking at these. It's impossible, seeing lives that continue to defy definition reduced to a checklist of bodily functions. But on the back of Mother's sheet, there's an open space in which Bernice writes down her own personal observations. This is where I see the words *nutsy fagin, distraught, frenzied.*

"My God, Bernice. What's this about? Where did you learn these words?"

"From your mother, Brenda. She's a walking dictionary.

But sometimes I don't understand, and I have to write them down. Then she tests me later."

"Tests you?"

"Yes. Like yesterday, we did *gar-ru-lous.* It means talkative."

"I know, Bernice. I know."

It's incredible, the devotion this increasingly irascible woman inspires among those around her. Aside from Bernice, my brother, and his estranged wife, Marie, there's the woman Mother calls St. Bernadette, an MSW with infinite reserves of patience who makes house calls. And the shrink who treats her to an endless supply of sample antidepressants. ("He's an old friend of Fannie Selleck, dear, the doctor who delivered you.") Then there's the fleet of home-care workers who deliver homemade soups and Portuguese rolls from a bakery in Danbury. All on their days off. There are even women who manicure her nails and massage her back. The whole house reeks of Ben-Gay the way it once did of Estée and Joy.

Many of them refuse to charge for their services. But I can't say they work for nothing. There's obviously something Mother gives them that brings them back day after day. As shrunken and ghostlike as she appears to me, Mom is still larger than life for them. Mother has been as removed from the modern world as those Stone Age tribes anthropologists discover hidden away in the jungles of the Amazon or New Guinea. This isolation has created an aura of authenticity and innocence around and about her that makes people long to protect her.

Sometimes, I think this attention is the only thing that keeps her alive. For sixty years, my mother lived in a state of perpetual panic, functioning on the same amount of adrenaline as those people you read about in newspapers who lift up a two-ton truck after an accident and pull out the bodies pinioned beneath it. Unfortunately, I'm not quite sure what Mom did with all that adrenaline when she was younger. Her organizational skills at home consisted primarily of setting the table for holidays like Easter four or five weeks in advance.

"Mom, it's February. What's with all the eggs on the dining-room table?"

"Well, I had a little extra time this afternoon. I thought I'd get a head start."

If there was any way she could have gotten away with cooking the dinner in February, she would have done it. Mother was immensely proud of her cooking. But her ignorance in the kitchen was almost as impressive as that of her sister Janet, who after forty years of living with her parents, the McLachlans, and eating food prepared by Pearl, the cook, walked into a Danbury grocery, pointed to the row of plucked chickens dangling from their necks behind the counter, and asked the butcher a perfectly logical question:

"What's the matter with those chickens, Louis?"

"Whad'ya mean, wassa matta' wid' 'em, Janet? They're the best chickens money can buy."

"I know that, Louis, but how come they only have two legs?"

"Ya' kiddin' me, right?"

"No, Louis. I thought chickens had four legs."

Either Janet had been seeing double all those years she ate at her parents' table (which was highly likely as she was an alcoholic), or when Pearl cut up a couple of chickens and served the drumsticks on a silver tray, she figured they all came from the same bird.

Cleaning was another one of life's unsolved mysteries for Mom. I know I never saw her make a bed or dust. Just the thought of operating household machinery made Mother drowsy or gave her a hernia. It was Dad who did the vacuuming. Like chipping paint off the outside walls of the house, vacuuming was how he handled his anger. Talk about sublimating. Feelings, dust balls, Mom's curlers — they all got sucked up into that Hoover. Alice Gregory cleaned, and Mrs. Gerow did the wash.

Mrs. Gerow was the McLachlans' Polish laundress. Twice a week, Mom drove the wash up to her house in Danbury. Mrs. Gerow was toothless and had black curly hairs that sprouted from the moles on her face. She stooped so low to the ground, she reminded me of the witch in "Hansel and Gretel." But I loved her kitchen. It was warm and moist from the washing. The windows were fogged up. You could smell the bleach, the hot iron, and her fresh-baked *babka* all at the same time. We packed the smell with us into the car along with our stiff starched sheets and inhaled it on the way home.

The kids' wash was usually done by Alice. The last time I saw Alice, she was lying in a blue satin-lined casket. Her face was all puffed up. I remember thinking how unlike herself she looked — not because she was dead or puffed up but because she was wearing my aunt Janet's shoulder-length platinum-blond wig. It seemed an odd choice for a seventy-four-year-old black woman. By then, though, I was pretty blasé when it came to looking at corpses.

In my years at the convent, dead nuns were very common.

We girls would line up in chapel and pay our last respects by sprinkling holy water on their faces. I didn't envy these women in their coffins. But I did envy their company, the people who loved them enough to stand by them and sing as they took that final hurdle into what I assumed would be a happier hereafter. I'd never heard such singing. It spoke not of our family's fears about life and death but of faith and of certainty. A certainty that the dead were about to leave their troubles behind and meet their Maker. For Alice, meeting her Maker meant looking her best. So perhaps the choice of a bright-blond party wig wasn't so odd after all.

One of the troubles Alice must have been delighted to leave behind was our Maytag. "I pulled the knob; that's all I done. I pulled the knob!" she wailed the day I found her cowering in a corner of the kitchen. Our Maytag wasn't just frothing at the mouth; it was churning its guts out, inching its way toward her across the floor. Poor Alice. Mother had used the washing machine as a hiding place for every liquor bottle in the house. It took the repairman hours, separating the splinters of broken glass from the suds and shredded remains of our underpants.

Hiding things was Mother's way of tidying up. No one could ever find the pots and pans. When they were dirty, she would open the oven or broom-closet door and shove them in. It was either that or soak them. Mother was a firm believer in soaking. Stuff would sit in the sink or on the counter "getting clean" for days.

She hid other things too. Like the Hefty bag full of Tiffany silver she took from Grandpa's after he died. She said she hid it under her bed because she was worried about burglars. The "burglars" were her two sisters. It wasn't greed that made my mother take it. It was rage and resentment. Her younger sisters had robbed her of her parents' affections, and this was her revenge. Like the silver, those feelings were never openly displayed. But she kept them as brightly polished as the tea set that Alice heaved out every month and sponged off with Gorham before returning it to its hiding place beneath the bed.

The Locke lawn mower she took was way too big to fit in a Hefty bag. For some reason, my mother imagined her sisters were as eager to have a three-hundred-pound lawn mower as she was: "Everyone knows this is the finest machine made," she boasted the morning it was delivered. "And thank God! There's no seat. You have to push it. Only lazy slobs sit on lawn mowers!"

The Locke was a perfect example of Mom hiding things when she didn't have to. Hiding, like lying, was a symptom of the deeper problem she had of revealing herself. Mom couldn't even tell time truthfully. She'd stare straight at her Timex and add or subtract up to twenty minutes either way. She lied about everything: from the real date of people's birthdays (the answer was always off by a day or two) to who she'd been talking with on the telephone.

"Mom, who was it?"

"Oh, no one you know. You wouldn't be interested."

I don't think she thought she was lying. She was keeping secrets. When I asked her once why she had kept even the slow and agonizing death of her own mother a secret from one of her oldest friends, a friend she had known since she was four years old and who found out that her mother had been sick only after reading the obituary in the local paper, Mom insisted that it was because she was a Scorpio. "It's one of our traits. Being secretive and passionate," she said. This was after my mother had been through twenty years of therapy.

Both of Mom's parents were "drunks." Although she never talked about it with us as kids, the abuse she endured as a child became her own private Alamo, a memory no less tragic in her eyes than the sinking of our ships at Pearl Harbor and the massacre of American Indians. In keeping her parents' secrets and covering up their sins, she lived with shame. And shame mutilates the spirit.

Mother says she survived the wounds of childhood. She "came out fighting." But she was also a martyr. In suffering, Mother found a sense of her own significance. She was a woman who defined herself almost exclusively in terms of what others had "done" to her. As such, she couldn't afford to forgive or forget. Seeking some kind of peace, unburdening herself of her secrets and her shame, would have meant a loss of identity. It would have been an act of submission synonymous with the appeasement pact Neville Chamberlain made with Adolf Hitler.

Secrets, for Mother, were a key to intrigue and power. Major or trivial as these pieces of information were — whether about the death of her mother or the time or the date of people's birthdays — the act of withholding them gave her some kind of leverage. It was like asking her if she'd read a book, seen a movie, eaten in a restaurant. She hadn't just read it, seen it, or eaten there. She'd done it all first. She'd "discovered" them just like she did the Indians.

"Oh! Your father and I knew about that place years ago. We lived there."

"Mom, you couldn't have. It only opened a month ago."

"I'm sure you're wrong. I remember it so well. . . ."

Hiding the facts of life wasn't quite so unusual for a mother back then. It was my aunt Janet who explained them to me. Mother's advice, however, was quite unusual. "Promise me you'll use Kotex and never, ever bring a Tampax into this house. I forbid it. They're horribly dangerous." Danger was a very real presence in our lives. As much as Mom tried to keep it a secret from us, we couldn't help but sense it.

When you're a child and you're told not to ride the plastic ponies in front of Woolworth because they might electrocute you, you listen. "They should be outlawed, banned!" This was her only comment when we pleaded for a dime to put in the slot. For Mother and for us, most of life's simple pleasures were fraught with peril.

She avoided nature like the plague, which wasn't easy considering it was all around us. This was because swallows, mice, rabbits, robins, and hamsters all carried the plague. "Mark my words," she'd say, pulling the curtains firmly shut on a glorious summer day. "They're absolutely vile! Filthy. They breed all kinds of disease." For her, the parade of children heading down to our pond to feed the geese at sunset was akin to the Charge of the Light Brigade. "Judas priest! Where are their parents? Those geese can beat a human to death with their wings. They're more vicious than swans." *Judas priest, holy sugarfoot,* and *crumbs of Paris* were as close as Mom ever came to swearing.

If a swan or swallow didn't get you, the weather would. "You'd have to be off your rocker to even consider going out on a day like this!" was her usual response to sunshine, snow, rain, fog, and sleet. Mom didn't just talk about the weather.

She stalked it. Every inch of her refrigerator ("icebox") door was covered with newspaper clippings that told the sad but true stories of people who died going outside: people crushed to death by their own trailers in tornadoes, frozen in their cars trying to escape blizzards, drowned by monsoons.

The taped-up clips only confirmed the obvious. You were better off never leaving your house. Never leaving your room and your bed would come later. The best policy was to stay indoors and take all necessary precautions. During thunderstorms, this meant unplugging all appliances, turning off all the lights, and not going anywhere near windows or the telephone: "Sorry, I've got to hang up," she'd say to friends the minute she saw a cloud.

Yet when it came to the biggest cloud of all, namely the nuclear one, she said nothing. It was incredible. There was a prefab bomb shelter for sale in front of Woolworth, right next to the electric ponies. Every time we passed it, I'd ask, "How much does it cost, Mom? Do you think it could really save us?" and she'd ignore me. Whether the silence was an attempt to shield me or proof that I had touched yet another nerve and that her own terror defied words of explanation or reassurance didn't matter. I spent years imagining precisely the possibilities she wouldn't acknowledge: from a slow and gruesome death due to radioactive fallout to instant annihilation in a single burst of lethal light.

The fact is, Mom was more comfortable keeping herself and all of us in the dark. Any real fears that were voiced on the part of a child — fears about the bomb, divorce, a dying grandparent — went unheard. Just as any real signs of physical illness, my sister's acute appendicitis, for instance, were shrugged off with a wet washcloth and a glass of ginger ale. Mom had memorized every symptom of leprosy, elephantiasis, trench mouth, and scurvy, but common, life-threatening illnesses like appendicitis went right past her. They hit too close to home.

It was denial. Denial, like hiding pots and pans, and a history of rampant alcoholism (her father, mother, sisters, Rhodie, and later Dad), and the facts of life, not to mention death, was the only way Mom could distance herself from a world of not-so-clear but ever-present dangers. She felt safe in the dark. Soothed by the voices of her friends on the radio, Dr. Atkins, Bernie Meltzer, Carlton Fredericks, Jean Shepherd, and surrounded by her books — my God, so many books — she was free to roam.

“don’t look! avert thine eyes.”

LIKE THE CRUMPLED-UP BALLS OF OLD NEWSPAPER THAT Larry uses to insulate his shack from the cold, this barricade of books that surrounds my mother began as emotional insulation — yet another wall that sealed her off from others but that as a child offered her solace and warmth. “My parents’ fights in the cellar were so bad; Daddy broke my mother’s nose a couple of times. I tried not to pay any attention. I delved into my books. But even when the help said it was nothing, I was a nervous wreck. Begging my mother to stop drinking only made it worse. She just pretended everything was la-di-da terrific. That was the beginning of all my fearfulness. Those nights I hid upstairs reading.”

When Mother told me this story recently, I wondered what her parents were doing down in the cellar. And then I saw myself spinning around and around on a red leather stool. This room where we had laughed and played as kids, but which for

Mother still echoed with the sound of her parents' muffled, furious screams, was a bar. It was a bar built by my grandparents during Prohibition. Hidden safely away from the prying eyes of curious neighbors and police, it was where they had secretly partied and fought.

To this day, Mother has never set foot in the basement of our house. Just mentioning it inspires the same aghast sighs with which she greets my news of trips to Shanghai and Moscow. But for thirty years, she's been sending an exterminator down there once a month. "Got another one!" the guy, Ray, would yell as he trudged up into the kitchen, toting a dead rat by its tail. "Looks like the same one from last month," Dad would say, poking the rat in its stiff, bloated belly. I'm sure my father was right. It was the same one. But it was memories and ghosts, not rats, that were scurrying around in Mother's subconscious. These were what she was hoping the exterminator would find a way to trap and dispose of in our basement.

After getting sober, her father, Arnold, transformed the cellar into a kind of Disneyland for us. There were hundreds of his model airplanes hovering from the ceiling and a table in the middle of the room with a network of Lionel trains. The trains whistled and belched steam when you put a pellet in their smokestacks. Watching us play with the trains and fill the dusty monogrammed glasses with the ginger ale we found in a tiny refrigerator hidden beneath the counter must have been intolerable for Mother. All traces of her Alamo, of the experience from which she never really recovered, had been erased.

Grandpa Arnold lost his leg at twenty-seven and devoted pretty much the rest of his life to cutting family members off at the knees. "I didn't find this out till I went spying around being a quisling," Mom would later confess. "But he broke his leg because his brother Jack made him have a race back to Colonel Serobin's. That was the riding club in Danbury. He was so drunk, he ran straight into a tree and fell off his horse. They were afraid he'd get gangrene."

Seeing that Brooks Brothers pajama leg pinned neatly over Arnold's stump as he hopped down the stairs on his crutches didn't exactly scare me. But it did stick in the imagination. I thought Rumplestiltskin and Arnold were related. "A banty rooster" is what my uncle Larry called him. He was as short as his temper, five foot five, give or take an inch, and as ornery as the proverbial wasp. Even on his deathbed, he couldn't resist a final sting. "Take those goddamn glasses off, Mary" were his last words. The priest was flabbergasted. So was Arnold's sister-in-law, Louise. Mother just smiled: "He's been this way all his life with me. Why should it be any different now?"

She was wearing her Woolworth sunglasses at the time. Her habit of putting them over her reading glasses drove Arnold nuts. So did everything about Mother: from her pop-it beads and perfume to her politics. "You're nothing but a fellow traveler, a pinko," he'd yowl at her across the dining-room table. "You bet your boots, I am," she'd spit back. "And proud of it!" Like one of those tiny grains of sand that embeds itself in the mucus membrane of an oyster, Mom went out of her way to irritate Arnold. This was how she got noticed. And she succeeded right up to the moment he expired.

Like my father years later, Arnold also loved flaunting his infirmity. "Christ almighty! What are you trying to do? Kill me? Can't you see I'm a cripple?" The sound of him pounding his crutch on the floor while he sat at his desk paying bills put the fear of God in everyone. Paying bills was a religious experience for Arnold. No one was allowed near his desk, with its battery-operated letter opener, its fountain pens, and its Brown Brothers checkbooks. It was an altar at which every member of the family but my mother came to bow their heads in prayer and give humble thanks.

Mother, as she liked to remind us at least twice a week, was a McLachlan, daughter and granddaughter of the men who had helped put Danbury, former hat capital of the world, on the map. In the thirty years before she was born, her granddaddy Harry, like old Mr. Potter in the movie *It's a Wonderful Life,* had controlled everything from the salaries that fed and housed the hundreds of Irish and Italian employees in his factories to their mortgages, light bills, schools, and savings accounts. Although her family's *fortunatus ad um* (this is what Mother called it) was minuscule compared to money created by industries like steel and oil and railroads, in a small blue-collar town like Danbury, the McLachlans must have seemed as rich and powerful as the robber barons.

"Don't look! Avert thine eyes," Mom would howl as we barreled past a discount toy store on our way home from the laundress, Mrs. Gerow, when we were kids. The store stood on the same spot as the mansion in which her grandfather Harry had lived with his wife, "Nanny West Street," and their seven children. "It was an atrocity, tearing that house down," she'd add, stabbing her finger at the blur of gleaming plate-glass windows that slid into the distance behind us. "That house was my history. My roots. And they've destroyed it. Just like they destroy everything else."

When I think back now to the scene of that "atrocity," how my mother repeated that same war cry each and every time we passed it, I know why she never really went anywhere. My mother's eyes were locked in the rearview mirror. Instead of receding into the distance, the objects that appeared in (more like blocked) her vision — her grandfather's house, her roots, her losses — only seemed to loom larger and larger over time. Even when Mom was tear-assing along a street in Danbury at sixty miles per hour, she wasn't looking at the road ahead. She was only looking behind her. The speed at which she attacked corners or parked and passed other cars may have given her an illusion of moving forward. But it was just that: an illusion.

In her sporadic fantasies of liberating herself from this sense of loss, of shedding the prickly skin that protected her as a McLachlan but that also exposed her to such pain, she dreamed of writing a novel about Harry and her family. This is where her spying around like a quisling and finding out about her father's horse accident began. In the beginning of the twelve notebooks she's crammed with research and writing about the McLachlans, she says that "Nanny West Street's real name was Margaret Byron. Maggie. She was Welsh and suffered from a malady that for years seemed to elude diagnosis or treatment but which kept her totally bedridden." Two of her children, Lorena and Isabelle, were daughters and five were sons: Harry, Jack, George, Donald, and Arnold.

"Blue-eyed, pink-cheeked, straight and stockily built; a quiet, genuinely modest man without an inkling about how to be spectacular." This was how Harry McLachlan was described in a speech given by a fellow hatter at the Hotel Commodore in New York in 1930. Mom keeps a copy of the speech in one of her notebooks.

Born a few miles from Glasgow in the town of Wishaw, Scotland, on March 3, 1870, Harry was the son of John

McLachlan and Anne MacDonald. "His father, John, was a gifted man," Mom writes. "A scholar educated in Rome who wrote both Greek and Latin fluently and who, at the age of twenty, was appointed secretary to the Duke of Argyll." Apparently, he was also such a severe and brutal drinker, his wife, Anne, eventually left with their children and returned to live with her family, the MacDonalds.

According to Mom, it was the MacDonalds who set sail across the North Atlantic and settled in New York, where Harry's grandfather resumed his occupation as a physician. No one knows why Harry and his mother moved north to the town of Danbury in 1883. Encouraged perhaps by the elder MacDonald's success as a doctor in New York or by the McLachlan family motto, *Fortis et Fidus,* courage and loyalty, their timing couldn't have been more perfect. The United States was on the brink of changes almost as turbulent and promising as those that would accompany Harry's own hormone-riddled leap into adolescence and manhood.

James Garfield had been assassinated, and Chester Arthur was the nation's twenty-first president. When I take my walks through Madison Square Park, I sometimes stop in front of Arthur's statue and run my hands over the smooth, cold surface of his foot and calf. The statue is hollow, but touching it brings me closer to this great-grandfather I never knew, to the boy who arrived in America just in time to read about the last performances of the Wild West Show with Buffalo Bill and Annie Oakley.

One year after leaving New York, Harry had moved on from a job selling handkerchiefs and gingham dresses at McLean Brothers, a retail dry goods store on Danbury's Main

Street, for a new, grittier job in the forming room of a local hat manufacturer, Beckerle & Co. Soon after that, he was foreman at Byron Dexter.

"A man's hat, no less than his house, symbolizes his culture and his place in the eyes of the world. Honest material and earnest labor in the making of the shelter and adornment of his head are no less important than the seasoned oak timbers of the house that he calls home." Archaic as this sounds, it says a great deal about the spirit and seriousness of the Scot who wrote it. These words were part of Harry's preface to a privately printed book entitled *The Making of a Man's Hat,* which was given to the thousands of men who attended that dinner in the ballroom of the Commodore at which he was the guest of honor. The photograph immortalizing that moment hangs dead center on Mother's wall.

Like her notebooks, the framed McLachlan family photographs that hang on the wall behind Mother's bed are as much an homage to her roots, to her pride in Harry and the hat capital of the world, as they are a reminder of how those roots have paralyzed her. Far from dead or buried, Mother clings to these ghosts and to the landmarks of her youth — a prosperous and thriving Main Street, with its Palace Theater, Danbury Men's Club, and Genungs Department Store — as tenaciously as we once clutched the life preservers Dad flung out to us on our maiden voyage aboard his vintage wooden motorboat.

There's Arnold speeding across Lake Candlewood at the wheel of his Chris-Craft; her uncle Jack lounging on a couch, cigarette and Scotch in hand; a stolid, unsmiling Granddaddy Harry in his three-piece suit and watch fob; and aerial shots of the McLachlan hat factories in Danbury and in Brookline,

Massachusetts. The only person missing in action, conspicuous by her absence, is my grandmother, Mary.

Mother claims Harry was "a benevolent despot. A man so revered people lined up for hours just to get inside the church for his funeral." She says he was good-hearted enough to pay the salary of every high school teacher in Danbury for a year during the depression. She was so proud of him and of his accomplishments, she wanted me to name my daughter Laurentia — "in honor of Dame Laurentia McLachlan. She was a Benedictine abbess, a cousin of your great-grandfather, and a good friend of Bernard Shaw."

Two afternoons a week, Mother would visit Harry and Nanny West Street at their mansion. "Aside from the cook, housekeeper, and two maids," Mom writes, "a registered nurse also floated among the various members of the family. Though her first allegiance was to Harry's infirm, crippled wife, she functioned as a family retainer." There was also a chauffeur, a man Mom says "performed the tasks of a general factotum." This "trusted Yankee driver" accompanied Harry everywhere, including the Sunday he set off in his Packard to rescue his son Arnold from the future that might have saved him.

"Unlike the girls, who attended either Manhattanville, in New York, or Trinity, in Washington, the boys in the family were free to choose their colleges. Daddy had chosen Brown and a career in law. But law, for Harry, was a heretical and harebrained scheme. Arnold, like all his sons, would finish college and come straight home to work in the factories. Arnold did what he was told. He transferred to Williams and then came home."

The sons, who were referred to by the help, the townspeople, and those who worked in their factories as Mr. Arnold, Mr. Donald, and Mr. Jack, lacked for nothing — cars, airplanes, horses, custom-built houses, and journeys abroad on English (and only English) liners. But their failure was the price Harry paid for his own ambitions and success. Failure for Arnold, Jack, and Donald came in the form of aimlessness and alcohol. Maybe it was power that went to their heads. Or inheriting and trying to inhabit hopes that weren't their own. Maybe unearned privilege, like abject poverty, automatically breeds this kind of aimlessness, an immunity to consequence.

Mother insists that "Arnold was a tough master and never missed a day at the factory, even if he was half in the bag." But he retired at forty-eight, and by the time I was born, all that seemed to be left of his family motto, *Fortis et Fidus,* was the solid-gold signet ring he wore on his pinkie finger, the coat of arms that hung in the front hall of his house at Ohehyahtah Place, and a bottomless bank account.

Mom would reject her father's money (and later her husband's) with the same vengeance her mother and sisters spent it. There was more to this rejection than rebellion or the pleasures of irritating him. When Mother was a child, money had made her feel excruciatingly conspicuous and guilty.

Unlike the children of Vanderbilts, Morgans, and Whitneys, who grew up in a rarified world far away from the mills, rigs, and mines that had made them, Mother lived with one foot in and one foot out of two radically different, polarized worlds — the world of privilege and power that had made her a somebody (or the daughter and granddaughter of a somebody, anyway) and the one outside it. Whatever unacknowledged feelings arose from the conflicts both within and between these two worlds would leave Mother as divided as the house she would later share with tenants and transient "dreamas" like Stan.

The world Mother encountered outside Ohehyahtah was no less terrifying or anxiety inducing than the one at home. It was full of men who paid a far higher price for Harry's success than his sons. Some were literally "mad as hatters." They'd gone insane from mercury poisoning. (Mercury was used in the finishing process.) Others suffered from lung problems after breathing in tons of loose rabbit hair, which was used in making the felt for Harry's hat bodies. Many of their children, the children Mother met at her elementary school, St. Peter's, were so poor she said they ate lima beans, and only lima beans, for Sunday supper during the depression. The school had a real-life Little Match Girl too. Her name was Lydia Batista. Mom would come home and cry because Lydia didn't have shoes.

It was Mother who confronted the envy and resentment of these men's children (and grandchildren) on her two-mile walks back and forth to school every day. "Daddy made us walk. But I didn't mind, really," she now says. "It was better than being stared at in the car with the driver." Mother walked even when kids threw rocks at her and called her a dirty scab. She thought a scab was something you pulled off your leg. She didn't know about strikes or that Harry and his sons had fought tooth and nail to keep the unions out of their shops. All her father said to her when she told him about how scared she was that morning was "Don't worry. They won't kill you for it, Mary. And if you sneak a ride home, I'll hear about it."

Mother's fondest memory of those years is of the help.

Along with the children she met in the novels of Dickens and Hugo, the help became her only allies. Mother had a particularly soft spot for Maddie, who worked in the kitchen; for the nursemaids; and for Henry and Hoover, who did the gardening. She detested Willie, the chauffeur — "He was a paid informant for Daddy" — and Nurse Nancy Jane Griffin. "She was sooo imperious. I couldn't stand her. She wore this starchy white uniform with a little winged cap."

Her parents' trips to the Carolinas for duck shooting or to Sea Island and Bermuda, where Arnold's brothers had houses, must have been the times Mother felt safest. Then and the day she packed her trunks and took off for the convent in Albany. When we were kids, Mother hid the secret of her parents' alcoholism as zealously as she did the Tiffany tea set she stole from their house and hid under her bed when her father died. "In the end, I had nothing but respect for my father and the way he handled that leg trip and gave up the sauce," she now says. "But they were all drunks in the family. Every single one of them except me and Aunt Lorena. That's why I couldn't wait for Lent. Everybody was sober for forty days and forty nights.

"I know I've told you this story a thousand times. Daddy flew me up to Block Island for lunch one day and had a few too many. He forgot to put down the wheels when we landed. I can still smell that smoke in the cockpit." Mom is craning her neck and pointing at a photograph of Arnold. Standing on the runway at Sadler's Airport in Danbury, he's wearing a tweed jacket and has one hand resting on the propeller of his olive-green Cessna. No wonder Mother always had such a rabid fear of flying.

But where was her mother when Mom left the house for Sadler's? Driving in a car with a drunk is bad enough. But flying? "She had no time for me. Period. She only had time for my baby sister. That's when she stopped drinking, you know. After she had her. All those years I pleaded with her to stop, she never listened. She didn't care."

My only souvenir of my grandmother Mary is on my dresser. It's a fourteen-karat-gold cigarette box. Her initials, *MMcL,* are engraved in diamonds in the top left-hand corner. Grandma kept her Camels in it on the nights Willie drove her and my grandfather down to the Cotton Club and Small's Paradise in Harlem. I had a brooch that was hers too — a heavy gold bow embedded with rubies and more diamonds — that was accidentally thrown down an incinerator chute.

Grandma's maiden name was Burns. She was twenty-eight, "ancient and Irish," Mom always said, when she married Arnold. Her father was a "merchant" who owned a department store in Norwalk called the Boston Store. "The McLachlans had a house on Belle Island and they all used to swim at Roton's Point in Norwalk. Your grandmother was a great swimmer. And so was your grandfather till he lost his leg. That's where they met."

Mary was everything Arnold was not — so supremely cool and aloof, it eventually gave her cancer. Mother called her Mrs. Marchmain, after the woman in *Brideshead Revisited.* My sister called her "the lady in the white house." Grandma wore Bonwit Teller tweeds, silk stockings with a seam in the back, and spectator pumps. Her hair, when it wasn't tightly coiled into a bun at the nape of her neck, fell all the way to her waist. Even when she was dying, she kept that hair. I behaved around

Grandma. We all did. When she poured me my spoonful of castor oil in the pantry, I swallowed it without a whimper.

Beneath her remote, unearthly air, I suspect there was a thin-lipped rage and an Irish wit so sharp-edged it could have cut through peat. Grandma lived in the lap of luxury. Once she sobered up, however, she would have been just as comfortable sitting on top of a stone pillar like those hermit saints in the Mideast or joining her sister, our great-aunt Mary Alice, at a nunnery in Maine. *The Education of Henry Adams, The Confessions of St. Augustine,* and St. Thomas of Aquinas's *Summa Theologica* were her favorite bedtime reads.

I don't remember her ever touching my mother or her husband, Arnold. "Shall I ring for Pearl, dear? Are you ready for dessert?" was the extent of their conversations. The only thing Arnold and Mary seemed to have in common was the one thing both preferred to forget: drinking. Once the drinking stopped, Grandma drove her car to Mass daily and to confession twice a week. She held bridge parties every Wednesday. Between rubbers, Pearl would serve iced tea and crustless cucumber, tomato, and watercress sandwiches. The rest of the week was spent in the service of others. I joined her for the trips to the hospital and to what Mom called "the booby hatch" over in Newtown, where we delivered Pearl's fruit pies and garden vegetables.

Even when she became mortally ill with lung cancer, my grandmother seemed taller than her husband. It was her carriage, her posture. People just automatically deferred to her. She treated death as yet another duty. Sheets and nightgowns were changed every day. Her hair got its usual one hundred strokes. She prayed and took her pills. All as penance and without complaint. Like many Irishwomen, Grandma mistook herself for a saint in the end. Her martyrdom left her daughter Mary cold. "I forgave her eventually, I guess. She was a lonely woman. Kept everything to herself. Books and the theater were her only comforts. She was very into upper-crust kinds of people. And she loved clothes. You've seen those pictures — how glamorous she was back in the thirties and forties."

The picture is in our den. Leaning up against a piano in her fur-trimmed evening coat and long white satin dress, Grandma was for me the epitome of class — as chic and mysterious as Greta Garbo. Even her house seemed to run as smoothly as the motorized chair that whisked her wheezing husband up and down the stairs. It was as neat as her bun and just as tightly coiled.

As the daughter of a mere merchant, or "a climber," Grandma also knew that facade, keeping up appearances, was important. Especially on holidays like Christmas. Greed is my own most vivid recollection of those Christmas-morning stopovers at Ohehyahtah. (We spent the afternoons at my other grandmother's house in Ridgebury.) We three kids would scramble out of the car, pushing and pinching one another, wanting to be the first to attack the pile of packages from FAO Schwarz, Tiffany, and Hammacher Schlemmer. Every box came exquisitely wrapped and tied with satin ribbons and a neat name tag. (Ours at home were wrapped by Mother in miles of crinkled-up Reynolds Wrap.) The grown-ups sat around on the couches, nibbling Planters cashews and undoing their own boxes so slowly and deliberately, it looked as if they were defusing bombs. There was no singing, no laughter, just tight little smiles and proper thanks-yous.

But the chintzes were perfectly faded and the leather-upholstered armchairs in the study nicely worn. White monogrammed towels hung in the black-and-white tiled bathrooms. (Towels, like sheets, had to be white. Grandma said color was "cheap.") In the summer, bouquets of flowers were picked fresh from the garden. The pencils had points, the cars had full tanks of gas, and the lowboy in the hall had a handy, never-ending supply of Arnold's white peppermint Life Savers. Only Mom seemed out of place. My first memory of her leaving the car running was when she dropped us off there on weekends.

It's inconceivable, even now, trying to reconcile the image I had of my grandmother with the one that haunts my mother, with a woman who had cut her oldest daughter off almost as deliberately as the doctors had amputated her husband's leg. "I remember the summer I came home from the convent and wanted to get a job. You were considered a total pariah if you worked in those days. And Mother was such a pill. 'You don't need a job,' she said to me in that hoity-toity voice of hers. 'Jobs are for people who need them.' "

Mom went straight down to the Danbury National Bank and introduced herself to the president, Mr. Jope. For the next two summers, she worked with the head bookkeeper, Mr. Frans, sorting through checks and filing them alphabetically. "Well, almost alphabetically. But it was an honor for me, working at that bank." When her mother insisted on picking her up in the afternoons, Mom made her wait in the car two blocks away from the bank. "I didn't want people to think I was a show-off. Or different from them, you know?"

It's amazing for me to hear my mother talk about a longing not to be noticed and to be like other people. What if I had known any of this earlier? Would it have made any difference in our relationship if I had understood that it was ambivalence that drove her to such furious extremes? that she was a woman as inflated by her own sense of self-importance as she was crippled by guilt and contradictions? But even a lifetime later, I wriggle in my chair at the thought of how just by opening her mouth, eating in a restaurant, or driving into town, this woman I called Mary, Mary, Quite Contrary somehow managed to mortify me.

"handicapped? what jackass invented that one?"

IN MY EARLY YEARS OF TRAVELING, THERE WERE NO DEATH-defying adventures — no perilous crossing of deserts or scaling of mountains, no war zones. Just the leap into other languages and the lives of those who spoke them. Juan Andres, Ulf, Gilles, Hans, Paki, Vincenzo. "It's like some goddamn foreign legion," Mom would say later. Mother couldn't even pronounce their names. And I loved it. As I chattered away to distant friends on the phone in Spanish or French, whispering and giggling, Mom would stomp around the kitchen, silently mouthing her words of fury: "It's rude, do you hear me? Rude! I don't want to hear another word of that stinking language in my house."

"Sorry," I'd say with my iciest, most supercilious smile after hanging up. "I forgot you never learned any languages." Abandoning my mother tongue in favor of Spanish, and later French and Italian, symbolized more than a rebellious streak or a rejection of Mom. Like ironing my hair with wax paper and wearing cookie-cutter clothes as a teenager, it was part of infiltrating and becoming one with the enemy. The enemy being, in Mom's eyes, anyone who lived in a world outside or other than her own.

The spring I turned twenty-one and flew back from Paris with my father, I began inviting the enemy home. "I'm a liberal," Mom would announce to these friends from abroad as we gathered in the den before dinner. "I'm a great fan of the underdog." The blank stares did nothing to deter her. Very few of these Peruvians, Venezuelans, Parisians, or Germans spoke English, which was a distinct advantage from my point of view. As she rolled merrily along, extolling the virtues of Cesar Chavez and of not buying grapes, I'd roll my eyes and tap my foot. The fact that the only real underdogs Mom knew worked for her or her parents was irrelevant. Pearl, the cook, Alice, who cleaned, and Hoover, the gardener, weren't underdogs, anyway. They were "family."

So was everyone who served, or rather "helped," her — the exterminator who, together with milkmen, dogcatchers, and casual passersby, also emptied garbage and changed lightbulbs; the telephone operators who were coaxed into interrupting phone calls with an "emergency" when she encountered a busy signal; and all the waiters at Fairfield County's inns and restaurants. Most of them appreciated, even enjoyed, her. For the uninitiated few, however, those new to her quirks, she was definitely the customer from hell.

Restaurants were the worst. "Good evening, Heinz." Heinz was the Bavarian headwaiter at our second kitchen annex, the Elms. "Nice to see you, Mrs. Cullerton. We have your table all ready." "Wonderful," said Mom, following him to her favorite corner. This was when one hand shot up as if to shield her eyes from a nuclear blast. "Would you mind removing that bulb in the wall sconce, Heinz? It's so bright, I don't know how anyone can stand it!" The five-watt bulb was unscrewed from its socket and gently placed in Heinz's jacket pocket. Next to go was the candle (the glare). And then, of course, the flowers (oxygen).

"Would you like a drink, ma'am?" asked the next victim.

"I certainly would, Max. I'd like a glass of water. From the tap, please. And don't forget to let it run. So it's cold. Oh, and one more thing. Please don't bring me one of those *huuuge* glasses you usually serve it in. I'd like it in a small, very small, juice glass. With no ice. Half filled."

This was Mother asserting herself. It was like going to the gas station. "Fill 'er up?" the innocent high school boy would ask as I shrank out of sight beneath the dashboard. "No, thank you. Two dollars, please. And don't forget the windshield." Five dollars was Mother's limit when it came to gas. Parking in illegal spaces — preferably those that blocked access to fire hydrants and stores or were reserved for the handicapped — was another means of self-assertion.

("Handicapped? What jackass invented that one? Everyone knows they like to be called cripples."

"But, Mom, we'll get a ticket."

"Not if you limp we won't. Go on. Limp.")

If Mom felt like parking in a no-parking zone or driving all over town with a dead man's license plates, it was her business. It wasn't that she didn't believe in the law. She did. She thought it should be applied rigorously and without prejudice to absolutely everyone. Except herself. She was very Italian that way.

She was, of course, also a McLachlan. And none of the usual rules or restrictions applied to her. The dead man's plates belonged to the recently deceased Arnold. They had his initials on them: AMcL. Why bother with all that rigmarole, reregistering her car at Motor Vehicles? It was so much simpler to just throw her own plates in the garbage can and ask the exterminator or the milkman to screw Arnold's on instead. Forget insurance. She drove without a license, anyway.

What mattered was that her dad's plates had "class." They were a vestige of the good old days, before chèvre and arugula, when license plates (along with everything else) really meant something. "They didn't give out initials to nobodies like they do now," Mom said with righteous indignation. "You had to be somebody big in the state, like Daddy."

But how big is a drunk who beats his wife? Mother seemed to forget this fact about her father as readily as she forgot the fact that she'd packed her bags the moment she heard he was sick in Danbury and gone into hiding at our apartment in New York until he died. Yet there she was, two days after he was buried, swiping his license plates and driving all over town with them.

The cops actually threatened to arrest her two months after she'd moved to New York. This was because she refused to "surrender" her auxiliary police uniform after a short-lived stint on the force. It was her version of "Cinderella," joining New York's finest. One tap of her nightstick and Mom was transformed from a phobic, middle-aged woman into a fearless savior of the streets, complete with badge, cap, and walkie-talkie. (Not that the streets around our apartment in Gramercy Park needed saving.) Perhaps being a cop, wearing a uniform, gave Mother a chance to throw her weight around, to be taken seriously by a world that too often made light of her.

She took it so seriously, she recruited me. I was twenty-four and had just started working part-time at an ad agency. My own stint with the auxiliaries lasted just long enough to get fingerprinted, which, as someone intent on keeping a low profile, I regretted before the ink had even dried. I remember my father ensconced in his orange leather chair with his feet up on an ottoman while I showed him how to subdue a suspect with my nightstick. My sister played the suspect.

"OK, Dad. First you get the perp to face the wall and spread his legs. Like this. Then you take your stick and put it between his thighs. Here, right under his balls."

"Uh-huh," says Dad.

"Then — this is the best part — you grab him by the back of the neck." Rachel was hopping around like a hobbled camel at this point. "And push. See? The guy can't even walk."

"Very effective, dear. I only have one question."

"Yeah?"

"How do you propose to get a 250-pound perp to stand up against a wall and spread his legs for you?"

"Shit. I didn't think of that."

"Well, I would if I were you. And while you're at it, think about either hitting him over the head, hard, or running like hell."

I never made it back to the precinct. But Mom was ecstatic about the whole experience. For a week. Then, like serving soup to the homeless with Mother Hale in the Bowery, the novelty wore off. For three months, the uniform hung in the back of her closet. She'd throw on an apron when she heard the doorbell and tell the officers she was the maid. "I so sorry, officer. The lady no here." It was the elevator man who "snitched" on her. As far as she was concerned, the city should have been grateful to her. She'd walked the beat (twice) and paid for the goddamn uniform. Why shouldn't she keep it?

It may have been transference, fighting crime in New York and serving soup to the suffering homeless while her father was dying in Danbury. But her withdrawal had to have been related to rage — the rage that is born of depression and that neglect, and only neglect, can nurture. But is it neglect that also nurtures narcissism? this tendency of my mother's to peer endlessly into her own reflection and to manipulate others through what is perceived as her helplessness?

It isn't my mother's helplessness, however, that gives me goose bumps when I listen to her speak now about her past. It is her pitilessness. Unable to forgive her parents' sins, my mother simply cut them off. Like Pal, who ran off to lick his own wounds in the woods, she withdrew. She withdrew into a world of fiction — both the fictions, the lies, she constructed for herself as an adult to make an intolerable and frightening reality more bearable and those created by writers like Poe, Dickens, Balzac, and Victor Hugo.

As a child, these were the writers whose novels must have mirrored and amplified the stirrings of half-formed feelings: feelings of anguish, sadness, anger, and guilt that she was forced to leave otherwise unspoken. Even as an adult, nothing cheered my mother more than her journeys into what she called "Stygian darkness. A world of misery and miscreants, of the sordid and the seamy."

Like her sympathy for the plight of Father Damien's lepers, Mexican grape pickers, and IRA hunger strikers, she identified with the suffering of the victims and the cruelty of the villains, with the callousness of a sadistic and dwarfish Daniel Quilp, with Uriah Heep, Mr. Gradgrind, Fagin, and the Man Who Laughs. But it was the powerlessness of the children — Pip, David Copperfield, Little Nell — that struck the deepest chord. Unlike the skittishness that defined her relationships with real people, with immediate family and friends, Mother would develop such an affinity for these nineteenth-century characters that many of them would spring from fiction into flesh and directly onto Ridgefield's Main Street. That's when we heard her shouts of "ingrate," "filthy cur," "swineherd," and "poltroon."

Mother took us with her on these journeys too. When she read to us for hours from *Great Expectations, The Little Match Girl, Oliver Twist, A Girl of the Limberlost,* and *The Secret Garden,* she was gazing into that rearview mirror. She was taking us back to her own backyard, revisiting memories of the depression, her loneliness, and those nights hiding upstairs. It was herself she saw in these sagas of the silent and the downtrodden, the forgotten and the crippled. This is why it was always the strange and the estranged, the afflicted, who appealed to Mother most and why she became such a magnet for misfits. She was one of them.

Death and deformity, whether physical or emotional, also fascinated my mother like nothing else in life. Tod Browning's *Freaks* was one of her top ten movies of all time. So was Buñuel's *Un Chien Andalou* and *Tristana,* the movie in which a one-legged Catherine Deneuve sleeps with her guardian. My only memory of her forty-eight-hour trip to visit me in Paris is of the two of us in a movie theater eating popcorn and watching Shirley Stoler in *The Honeymoon Killers.* She had no interest whatsoever in seeing the Eiffel Tower, the Louvre, or, God forbid, the French. The French were "collabos," no better than the "bloody Boche, the Huns."

She preferred to see a matinee about American murderers or to hole up in a hotel room with books about the Siamese twins Chang and Eng, the bearded ladies, midgets, the elephant man, and geeks. Mother knew everything there was to know about these misfits and freaks but very little about the run-of-the-mill humans who gawked at them.

As a kid, I shared her fascination with freaks, and I couldn't wait for our demon-seeking in the dark. Mother could feel things in the dark that were obscured and impossible for her to grasp in the light of day. What denial had taught her as a child to tactfully ignore, reading made real again. Words made my mother weep. I can still hear the strangled sounds of her sobs as she read to us from the last chapter of *The Wind in the Willows.*

When Mother read, she forgot to be afraid. Books gave her wings. They moved her in ways the outside world never would or could. As she led us into the London underworld, with its prisonlike orphanages, or down the dismal passages of a French coal mine and across the seas to the land of Kipling's Raj, I could hold her hand. I could lay my head in her lap. I could show her that she wasn't alone and that I loved her. I loved being with her on these voyages that took us so far away from home.

Best of all, books were also something she shared with her husband. Books brought my parents together the way church, sex, and the PTA did others. When Dad touched down from his faraway places, he always arrived bearing gifts of jewelry and books for Mother. Mom didn't give a damn about the jewelry. She wore the gold and diamonds with her pop-it beads and her underpants when she gardened.

The most peaceful moments between my parents seemed to be in those hours just after dawn when they sat together in the den, sipping coffee, tearing cartoons out of the *New Yorker,* and chatting about their books. The two of them even took turns reading out loud to each other in bed at night. Listening to the wave of words, to the gentle rise and fall of voices down the hall, I'd snuggle under the covers and think: *Aha! So this is what it means to be a grown-up.* The thought of interrupting them never occurred to me. Reading out loud seemed as intimate and private an act as making love.

Stretching out to fill that voluptuous space before my own plunge into obliviousness and sleep, I'd forget that I was afraid. Afraid of the bomb and of seeing my mother laughed at, afraid of the arguing that would come when Dad took off again, and afraid of not being noticed when I slid beneath the water of the bathtub and floated there, holding my breath with my eyes wide-open, wondering if this was how it felt to be dead.

Most children assume they will live forever. Not us. Not me or my mom. I have a photograph of her when she was eight or nine. It was taken by her father at about the same time that she was overhearing the drunken brawls in the cellar. Sitting on a chintz couch and wearing steel-rimmed spectacles and a Liberty cotton dress, she had just returned from a one-week stay at the Lahey Clinic in Boston.

Her fears and the fighting in the cellar had tied her stomach into such terrible knots, she couldn't stand up straight. Like the hump she now has on her back, the burden of sadness and secrets had her doubled over. Nothing the doctors told her could dissuade her from this conviction that she was dying. At an age when other girls dream of becoming ballerinas and princesses, my mother was already busy digging her own grave. Yet there she is smiling, lying for the man behind the camera, the man who had broken the bones of her mother's nose and splattered her blood on the cellar floor.

Seeing that snapshot now, Mom looks so forlorn and solitary you want to reach out and hug her. This is the tragedy — that so few ever did. Mother never came out from hiding. She never grew up. Sure, she went through the motions: college, marriage, kids. But her efforts met the same dismal fate as the swallows that crashed into our dining-room windows. There were faint flutters of hope. "Up the Reb!" I'd hear her mutter to her reflection in the bedroom mirror. Dressed in a jumpsuit covered with a jungle print of giant neon ferns, she'd set off to conquer the evening like an exotic, deformed bird — a bird born without wings.

When I ask my mother now why she isn't reading, why the books that once opened windows into so many wider worlds are shut, she says she can't, that words make her feel nauseated and disoriented. Unlike Dad, my mother is utterly defenseless without the words and books that once defined and sheltered her. Even the lights in the house are on twenty-four hours a day now. "Just like Motel 6," she says, making a feeble joke about her newfound terrors of the darkness and the night.

"so this is how it feels to be famous?"

I'M THE ONE WHO SEEMS TO HAVE INHERITED MOM'S compulsive reading habit. And it's so out of control at the moment, Richard jokes about sending me into rehab. He's even made me a T-shirt that says "Why Read When You Can Skim?" The restrictions I once imposed on myself to curb the habit — sticking to newspapers and magazines before the sun goes down and reading books only after the children have gone to bed — have totally disintegrated. I'm devouring up to three, even four hundred pages in broad daylight. I'm obviously depressed.

Reading is a drug. It puts me into a kind of listless stupor. It insulates and isolates me, just as it did my mother. I feel so guilty about feeding the habit, I hide shopping bags from Barnes and Noble in the bottom of the garbage can and bury new books in the middle of the stacks around my bed, hoping Richard won't notice them. The astigmatism in my left eye is getting worse. I can feel the strain on the muscle. I read with one eye shut to give the muscle a rest.

Sometimes, I feel as if I woke up one morning at the age of forty-six and my life went blank. It crashed. Until that morning, a year ago, life was something that happened to me, something I could respond and react to. Now there's nothing. Nothing but this goddamn computer and the visits to Ridgefield.

What am I doing, strangling in the roots of my own backyard, so entangled and enmeshed in my parents' lives, my skin breaks out in red welts? They itch. But when I scratch, they bleed and leave scabs. "It's probably hives," my doctor tells me. I think it's living in my parents' skin. It's all the waiting and worrying, the shuttling not just between their houses but between these periods of comic relief and disbelief, of intensive caring, apathy, and callousness. I'm literally itching to get rid of them.

But instead of getting help and talking to a shrink, I've turned to horoscopes. I'm obsessed with horoscopes. They reassure me. Even if my forecast is lousy and my moon is in major retrograde with Mars opposing Pluto, they remind me that something is about to happen; something is about to change.

Something is happening, of course. Dad's condition is getting steadily worse. He sleeps a lot. Not even the crinkle of an aluminum wrapper around a Hershey bar snaps him out of it. It's been four months since the January morning when paramedics lowered him down from that ambulance on a gurney. "Surprise!" he'd said with a cackle. "I'm baaack!" Dad had lost virtually everything by then except his sense of humor.

I wish I could say the same for Mother. There is a deepening desperation to her phone calls, and it takes a tremendous amount of energy and effort to pick up.

"Your brother has confiscated my car keys!" I can hear her sobbing on the machine from my kitchen before I run in and grab the phone one Sunday afternoon.

"I know, Ma. I heard."

"I was taking a shortcut to your father's."

"Through the pine trees? Over the lawn?"

"It's quicker."

"Geoff says you ran over a boulder. There's a hole the size of a basketball in the chassis."

"You don't understand. I need that car. I need to drive again."

"I do understand, Ma. I do. But you have to get a little stronger, that's all."

No one can believe this woman somehow hauled herself out of bed, down the steps, and into the front seat of her Oldsmobile. "There was just the nose of the car, poking through the bushes," Geoff tells me. "I thought I was hallucinating." The wheels were whirring. She was gunning the engine and sitting on the horn. "Jesus, Mom. Where the hell do you think you're going?" he screamed. "I'm coming to visit," Mom yelled back. "Yeah. Well, from now on you can call first. We'll come and get you."

By the time Mom hangs up, the inertia is settling over her again like a dense, heavy fog off the Grand Banks. I feel so sorry for her. I don't understand why she's in such a hurry to get to the back house to visit Dad. Being a prisoner in his own backyard has done nothing to bring my father closer to his wife. There are times I've wondered why the rupture of that tiny vein in his head didn't wipe out his anger the same way it did most of his memory and his cravings for nicotine and booze. Instead it only seems to have distilled it, to have reduced it to its vitriolic essence.

"So how's Ma?" I used to ask him, offering him the cue for a response I already knew by heart.

"Pe-cu-liar, you know what I mean? Cunning, devious."

Dad would cock his head and blink like a parrot, then give me that thumbs-down gesture the Romans used to signal their desire to see a gladiator die.

"You're the one who's peculiar," I'd answer with a sigh.

"You bet your ass. I'm entitled."

"Can't you even try to be nice to her?"

"Fuck her. No way."

I'll probably never know if the war that broke out between my parents so long ago was triggered by my father's drinking and his increasingly frequent departures or by Mother's own disappearances, her vanishing acts into depression. Depression, like drinking, has always seemed to me to be a form of disappearance. "Periods of feeling utterly diminished, rudderless," is how Mother describes it. But the fifty feet of driveway that separates my parents today reminds me of the green line on the island of Cyprus that separates the Greeks from the Turks.

When I walked across that razor-wired no-man's-land on a trip to Cyprus in 1988 and passed the Ledra Palace Hotel, pockmarked with bullet holes and long since abandoned, I wondered if the gun-toting soldiers, manning the guard booths at either end, might have once lived in the same village and known one another's families. Fourteen years after the civil war, a war the locals still referred to as "the troubles," the wounds of the Cypriots lay as close to the surface as the shards of amphora and chunks of polished white marble that glittered beneath the surface of the waters where I swam near the ancient city of Salamis.

Unlike my parents' house, the schizophrenic division of the island had created a paradise for tourists like me on the Turkish side. For three weeks, I wandered alone through the dunes of this fabulously forgotten city: birthplace of Venus and Aphrodite, Hadrian's favorite vacation spot. Tufts of grass pushed their way up through great granite columns in the amphitheater, and snakes sunned themselves on the broken pipes that once fed springwater into the vast complex of Roman baths. What conspiracies and intrigues, what secrets, were shared in those retreats into steam and stone so many centuries ago? I wondered. Wading into the mosque-blue sea, I could touch the remnants of the breakwater that had sheltered ships heading for Syria, Palestine, and Rome.

For me, the most haunting ruins of all in Cyprus weren't the crusaders' castles or the Greek and Roman temples but the empty houses from which the Greeks had fled just over a decade before. Although my affinity for the damaged, my attraction to such desolate, divided places, was hardly new, it was too easy to imagine the panic of grief and frenzy here, the fear that had forced these families, with their aunts, uncles, and grandparents, to run.

Did they send their children out to play while they stayed inside to pack? Did they fight over what to take? Did they gather up practical things like pots and pans and blankets? Or, like Mother, did they only make room for the past in their futures, cramming old photographs, bits of silver, and letters into battered trunks?

I had always sought out cities from which others had fled, once-upon-a-time capitals of empires that had been ransacked, looted, left for dead. For me, the magic of Aleppo, Havana, Beirut, and Trieste lay in everything that was missing, in the absence of whatever lavishness might have once made them rich and complacent. But these Greek ruins weren't cities or empires. They were small villages, intimacies interrupted, and private lives blown apart by the burden and the weight of memory.

If these houses had been destroyed by the Turks, burned to the ground, it would have been less disturbing. Instead they were simply left to rot, collapsing in on themselves in heaps of dusty plaster, broken glass, straw, and wood. They were dying from neglect. The depth of my response to those ruins in Cyprus, the freshness of the wounds, and the feelings of scrapped-out hollowness inside had to have come from a place closer to home.

It wasn't a question of being conceited enough to think I could slip into the skin of a Turk or a Greek Cypriot that had me drawing these emotional parallels between this island and my parents' home. It was seeing how, just like at home, time had done so little to heal the wounds here, and that conflict, again like at home, had forged a connection between these people that was more intense and addictive, more passionate, than peace would ever be.

It was seeing these seemingly minor acts of neglect. Leaving houses to decay and collapse, houses that had once been alive with the smell of cooking and the noise of children, was such a personal, domestic act of war — much uglier and more grotesque for me than the occasional glimpse of a neatly uniformed soldier carrying a gun and manning a guard booth.

I saw nothing benign about this neglect. Just as I saw nothing benign in my father's reluctance to part with a penny to pay for repairs to Mother's roof, to mow the meadows that once were lawns, to maintain a property divided in half by unresolved hostilities. There was a time when this house was as pretty as a picture, when people would stop at the bridge down by the pond and get out of their cars to photograph and sketch it.

It infuriates me — seeing everything falling apart. It's not just small things like the doorknob that comes off in your hand when you turn it and that would need only a few new screws to fix. It's more important things like the front stoop. The concrete that holds the stones together is crumbling, so half the steps are missing. You have to clutch the railing and make zigzagging goatlike leaps over the holes to get in the door.

I know that we are hard up for money, that we have bigger things on our minds. Like the fact that our parents are falling apart. Dying. But being here and seeing the remains of a world torn apart by its own far-from-civil war — a war that has left my brother living in a tar-paper shack and all of us battling either addictions or depression — leaves me feeling utterly defeated. This collapse of our outer world goes far beyond anything I could ever attempt to fix as conservator. Because it isn't due to normal wear and tear or to casual carelessness. It is the cumulative effects of neglect that have created this no-man's-land of the dead and the dying.

Two months ago, I found a corpse out in the barn. It was a guinea hen. Geoff had bought four of them from a farmer over in Brewster. They were a "short-term solution" to getting rid of the deer ticks. Stroking their long speckled feathers as they tumbled out of the car, I thought about how cute, how soft and silky, they were. Their pinheads, peck, peck, pecking their way across the yard, and their bloodcurdling screeches had us all in hysterics.

What Gordon described as "God's music" soon had the neighbors up in arms. They couldn't stand the noise. Geoff, who grew tired of rousting them out from beneath bushes and down from tree branches at dusk and of getting up at dawn and chasing after them with a broomstick and a fishing net, banished them into a pen in the barn. And that's where they'd been ever since. The one I found had been the first to weaken. It was eaten by its comrades.

To make an analogy between the way we were cared for as children and the fate of these guinea hens would be a monstrous exaggeration. But there is something about our experiment with the guinea hens that's frighteningly familiar.

As teenagers, we didn't chase cars like Pal. We crashed them. But just like Pal and all our pets, whose carcasses were left to rot in the woods, our battered Volvos, Mazdas, and Fiats were abandoned right where they were — wherever they happened to meet their untimely demise. And there they'd sit on a New York street or a Massachusetts turnpike until somebody stripped, auctioned, or towed them off. "Grossly irresponsible," most people said. But these acts of recklessness and abandonment might have also been an echo of our mother's war cries. An echo of her plea to be seen and heard, to be taken care of.

Yet how could a woman who was so afraid of lightning she slept in rubber boots, thinking they would ground her, send her children out into the rain and snow half naked? We were told to take turns wearing mismatched hats and gloves. This was the paradox. Far from overprotective, Mother's attitude toward child rearing was as casual as her housekeeping. No matter how perilously close we came to self-extinction, she just didn't seem to notice. If, as a toddler, I felt like peddling down three flights of stairs on a tricycle, I did. (It was the garbage-man who gently wrapped me in blankets, picked me and my severed finger up, and carried me to the car.) If I felt like swimming in a hurricane, that was OK too.

The hurricane incident took place in the spring. I was twelve. Mom had decided to whisk us all down to Ft. Lauderdale on a Greyhound bus. Her flying days had come to a grinding halt in 1962. "Don't ask me how your father talked me into going down to that hedonistic hellhole." (The hellhole was Nassau.) "But on the flight back, I kept asking the stewardess where we were. That's when your father lost his temper. 'For God's sake, Mary. We're in the air. Up in the sky. Now shut up.' When we landed he told me he would never, ever set foot on another airplane with me again. 'Ha!' I said. 'I beat you to it, Bob. Because not only am I not flying with *you* again, I'm never flyin' anywhere again.' And that was it. I never did."

Mom had broken her pinkie toe right before the trip to Florida. She was hardly a stoic when it came to physical pain. She told the driver numerous times to slow down on curves and bumps. But this wasn't some McLachlan limousine driven by Willie the chauffeur. It was a fully loaded public bus on a schedule. With Mother no longer able to bear the pain (mostly of being ignored), we got off at four o'clock in the morning in Jacksonville.

With no taxis (or stretcher bearers) available, Mom bribed a porter to wheel her on one of those stand-up luggage trolleys from the station to the best hotel in town. The drunks we passed along the way must have taken a heavy slug of the old Night

Train, seeing this woman as stiff as a cigar-store Indian, careening down the street at a forty-five-degree angle and moaning, "My toe. My toe!" The hotel was great. We got to order iced hot chocolates from room service and watch TV, while Mom lay in the bedroom planning her future in traction.

As for the hurricane . . . The red flags, the pounding surf, the upside-down lifeguard stands meant nothing to Ma. She figured we were as immune to drowning as we were to pneumonia. "I'll keep the heat on, kids," she promised when we jumped out of the rental car for a dip. The current was so strong, it ripped my bathing suit off. It was the police who rescued us. After a quick motel shower, we were put on the last glass-bottom boat up the Everglades. "You can watch the Seminoles wrestle alligators while I nap," Mom said.

Naptime was the only steadfast rule at home and away. We had to stay in our rooms for two hours every afternoon. What we did in that room once the door closed was our own business. "Couldn't you two find anything better to do?" Mom asked with an exasperated shrug the day I chopped off all my sister's hair. Rachel had sat patiently in the wicker laundry basket while I scalped her. For two months, she walked around looking like the girl in *Ryan's Daughter.*

Rachel retaliated by sticking wads of chewed-up Bazooka bubble gum in my braids. When the two of us appeared at our grandmother's English Christmas, sporting our few remaining tufts of hair, there were gasps of utter disbelief. "Oh, Mary! Mary! Such beautiful heads of hair. How could you let this happen?"

For Mother, it was a detail, something to be dismissed as lightly as the border between the United States and Canada or swimming in a hurricane. It was like the night my brother returned from two years of school in France at the age of seventeen and hitched a ride from the airport only to find his house empty. Really empty. We'd moved. Forgetting to send him our new address was another detail. Mother herself had never set foot in the new house — not until Dad unpacked the boxes and made it home. It was the old Lockwood place, wasn't it? She'd seen it once or twice in passing from the car window.

For many sailors, the first three blasts of a ship's whistle that signal departure and the long single blast later as she clears the harbor mark the beginning of a journey not away or ahead but back. Back to the home they're always leaving behind. I never had such romantic or poetic illusions about my childhood home. That rainy night when Geoff peered through the windows and pounded on the door of an empty house confirmed it. We were transients. All of us. Our lives were interminably long and torturous games of hide-and-seek, with everybody hiding and nobody seeking.

It was no metaphor, this game of hide-and-seek. It was as real as the wall that split our house in two — as real as Mother hiding in her room, shoving pots and pans into closets, liquor bottles into washing machines, and the family silver under her bed. It was as real as my father hiding out in hotels around the world, at our apartment in New York, and at the house at Lake Candlewood, and burying a hoard of cash inside the toes of moldy old shoes before sending us out to find it armed with nothing more than vague hopes and a map scrawled on a hospital napkin.

I once heard that children who play hide-and-seek, like toddlers who play peekaboo, learn to fear abandonment less, that through repetition and by taking turns being hiders and seekers, they learn that someone will always come to find them. "Bullshit," as my father says fifteen times a day. Life, at least in our houses, just didn't ever seem to work out that way.

Perhaps that's why, as a kid, I dreamed of being "discovered," of becoming a star. All I ever really wanted was to be found, to be hugged and held as I lay on a concrete floor after peddling down three flights of stairs on a tricycle or as I sat huddled under my grandmother's winter coats in the cedar closet, quietly waiting for the sound of footsteps that never came. Instead, using a broomstick as a microphone, I'd put "Funny Girl" or an Italian 45 called "I Watusi" on the record player in the den and sing along at the top of my lungs. Swaying to the music, I'd close my eyes and imagine the crowd, clapping and stomping their feet, shouting for more of me.

Strangely enough, my fantasy of fame did eventually come true. Two days after my experience in the hospital in China, I was in a sports stadium on the outskirts of Dalian. The crew on the *QE2* had challenged the locals to a soccer game as a goodwill gesture before the ship sailed on to Japan, and thirty thousand Chinese had packed themselves into the bleachers. But our team had drunk so many liters of Snowflake beer and rice wine, they were almost unconscious. As they struggled valiantly on toward slaughter, a group of cheering crew members leapfrogged over my head and dashed out onto the field.

Weaving past each section of the bleachers, the men took a number of sweeping, inebriated bows. The crowd went crazy. Next thing I knew, I had joined them. Deafened by the sound of thirty thousand applauding fans, I was dizzy. After bowing with my arms outstretched, I was hoisted into the air and carried off the field on the shoulders of Manchurian soldiers. *So this is how feels to be famous?* I thought, throwing kisses to the crowd. *To be loved like Barbra, Mick, and Janis.*

But I didn't become famous. I kept on moving. Three days after my wedding, I even took off on a honeymoon to the South Pacific, alone. How many women honeymoon alone? I hadn't exactly planned it that way. The night before our departure, Richard decided to stay behind and direct his first rock-and-roll video. But flying off into the distance a mere three days after I had stood at an altar and taken my marriage vows wasn't just a last hurrah for independence at thirty-two. My vanishing act, the sudden rupturing and severing of ties, must have been a means of reliving the transience, the tenuousness, of those connections that had shaped me as a child.

It was after my three-month honeymoon (Richard eventually met up with me in New Zealand) that I came back to New York, pitched the proverbial tent, and became a nomad, an advertising freelancer who continues to develop slogans for the ever-transient hordes of fashion. There is no greater luxury in the world than being paid to think. But it's strange, that I should have stumbled into a world devoted so entirely to appearance and facade, and even stranger still that I frequently provide the text for books on the home.

I also became a professional ghostwriter. Being paid to put words and feelings into powerful people's hearts and mouths is a perfect fit for someone who prefers to remain invisible and who slips so easily into people's skins. For too many years, I've blamed these clients for taking my bows, for keeping me in the shadows. You'd think I'd know that I was playing another game of hide-and-seek, that I have chosen to be a ghost precisely because, like when I am speaking other languages or when I am working with one foot in and one foot out of so many different worlds, I am safe. No one can touch me.

Dad at twenty at Dartmouth

“why does your father want to kill kenny?”

THIS ACHE TO RETURN TO THE *QE2* AND OTHER OCEAN liners, to those quiet mornings lying in a wooden deck chair while stewards tucked my toes into the neat, tidy corners of a rough blue blanket and served me hot bouillon and tea, is as close as I ever come to feelings of real nostalgia. “To be at sea” usually implies a negative, as if being unmoored were somehow a sin. But similar to jet lag, that sensuous fatigue after a long-distance flight when the body is neither here nor there and longs only to sink into sleep, the sea for me was a blissfully tranquil place. It was a place in between, neither here nor there, where others like me, who lived with one foot in and one foot out, finally felt at home.

I still keep in touch with friends from these ships who’ve run aground and been forced to retire. Daniel Kenworthy, former engineer first class, is one of them. Orphaned during the London Blitz and raised by his “aunties” in Liverpool, he’s been marooned in the village of Dreemskerry on the Isle of Man since the *QE2* switched from boilers and steam to diesel more than a decade ago.

I met Daniel in a Force 7 gale on the North Atlantic. I was seventeen, crossing from New York to Southampton. It was he who introduced me to the secret society below five deck that for the next fifteen years kept both the ship and my dreams afloat. Through Daniel, I became friends with deckies (deck-hands), chippies (carpenters), and sparkies (electricians). While passengers lazed about in the Double Down Room or jogged on the Lido deck, I stood in awe and a pool of sweat as asbestos-clad men crept into the bellies of six-story boilers to clean out tubes. "The jaws of hell," Daniel called it. Three minutes was the maximum any man could stand it.

Daniel told me I'd need a blowtorch to free up the davits that secured the lifeboats on deck. That's how rusted they were. "You'd be safer crossing the seas on *Kon-Tiki,*" he'd say with a smirk. But I felt as happy and privileged donning a boil-ersuit or eating homemade curry cooked in a coffee can on a Bunsen burner in the carpenter's shop as I did wearing silks and sauntering into the Princess Grill for champagne and caviar. Ships were the symbol of all that it meant to be *away.* Anonymous. "Where are you going?" friends would ask, wait-ing to hear the name of a city or country as they saw me off from the dock. "Just away," I'd say. "Far away."

How can I explain this addictive hold, this passion, I have always felt for the far away? The fact that my father seemed to prefer a life that was faraway, that he found some kind of hap-piness there that eluded him here, and that I tried to follow in his footsteps, is part of it. "Why does your father want to kill Kenny?" a nurse came up and asked me the last time Dad was in the hospital. "He's been saying 'Kill Kenny, kill Kenny' for hours." Kilkenny is a place, not a person. It's a town in Ireland he used to stop and visit on his way back from Europe. Two months ago, it was Ischia, Capri, and Rome that had him misty-eyed. "Ahhh, 's a wonderful place. Superb," he'd say, looking out at his backyard and seeing the Spanish Steps, the Bay of Naples, and the faces of the women he picked up along the way who gave his life as a drifter some sort of direction. If only my father had been less driven. Then, perhaps, the fact that he never had a destination wouldn't have destroyed him.

But when he was young, my father personified the romance of flight. It was he who inspired my dreams of taking off at a split-second's notice without even stopping to book a seat. (Dad's travel agent wrote out stacks of prepaid tickets, which he kept, along with a pile of traveler's checks and fistfuls of foreign currency, in a drawer upstairs in his bedroom.) Dad was my Marco Polo, an explorer literally pulling jewels out from his pockets while he told exotic stories about the foreigners he met along the way. I lived inside these stories just as I did my favorite Greek myths. Because there were so precious few of them, I wanted to hear them over and over again.

One of his best stories was about the rock-and-roll musician he chatted with on a flight across the North Atlantic. "Is he famous, Dad?" my sister impatiently asked. "You must know if he's famous."

"Yes, I think he is," Dad said with a grin, fumbling around in his wallet for a scrap of paper. "Aha. Here it is. He asked me to call him."

The guy was Keith Richards. Dad took him and his son to dinner and a hockey game in town a couple of months later.

Then there was the story of his crack-of-dawn flight into

Rome when he discovered he'd forgotten his passport. He called the American embassy and somehow talked his way straight through to the ambassador. The ambassador roused himself out of bed, pushed the papers through, drove them out to the airport, and offered Dad a ride back into town. "How, Dad? How the hell did you do it?" I asked. "Well, the guy was a marine, just like me," was his only explanation.

I also shared my father's fascination for the Clarks, an English family with names like Bancroft, Brooking, Lancelot, and Galahad. Immensely rich but pathologically low profile, the Clarks were Quakers. While Dad flew only first class and via the Concorde, the Clarks flew only on Freddie Laker and People Express. They lived in Street, a "dry" town in Somerset, where alcohol at the local inn was kept under lock and key, but the doors to everyone's houses were open twenty-four hours a day.

It was sixty-five-year-old Nathan Clark who showed me how to squirt water from wooden nickels while regaling me with tales of being in India during the last days of the Raj, of patrolling the Northwest Frontier in the company of giant Pathans, of building the Burma Road, and of chatting with Jack Rose Smith, the man who later became my father's mentor at Clarks, in a foxhole where it was raining bullets.

Nathan's townhouse in New York had a swimming pool in the middle of the living room. He would invite ballet dancers over to do laps. I wondered whether Nathan's pool and his support of the arts and dance had less to do with his philanthropic impulses and more to do with other impulses. But his intelligence, his energy and experience, enthralled me.

Catching up with my father in his travels, meeting the Clarks and his friends in these grand hotels all over Europe where everyone seemed to know his name, was about being faithful to him. The rootlessness, that feeling of being at home and hopeful only when far away . . . it was a bond we shared. What Dad never had time to tell me was that the act of flight doesn't necessarily have anything to do with moving forward or creating a future.

I have always been terrified that if I am caught looking forward to the future, it will be snatched away from me. There are times now when I think that if I had stayed and talked to that shrink John Brooke when I was eighteen and first suffered the physical symptoms of my phobias, the swollen glands and dizziness, I might have been cured of these afflictions — these terrors that, like my mother's, must be the echoes of depression.

But that's when I also think of what I would have missed, of the houses in countries far away that even if occupied for the space of a meal or a month became a part of me. When newfound friends in Europe first invited me to stay as a guest in these houses and I learned that many of them had been inhabited by the same families for centuries, that generation after generation of children had returned to the same rooms in which their parents and their parents before them had grown up, I felt a vicarious thrill. It was, I think, the thrill and the possibility of belonging.

So I used my memories of these houses to create an imaginary home in my head. The joy of "owning" a home like this is that, unlike other homes, it travels with me everywhere and boasts an almost infinite variety of rooms. They are rooms in which I am always welcome and to which I return whenever my world as wife, mother, and sibling becomes too small for me.

It is usually when I am plagued by fits of insomnia, when I am so restless that not even reading quiets the jumpiness, that I close my eyes and begin to wander through the labyrinth of rooms in this "other" house of mine. The first stop is a bedroom exactly like the one in a stone house near Le Puy, France. It was here that I slept on my first pair of linen sheets in a Venetian sleigh bed. The bedcovers were made of slippery rose-colored silk, and painted cherubs cavorted in the clouds above my head.

On the ground floor, I have a dining room just like the one I remember visiting in a mansion on the shores of Lake Geneva. The table is an immense slab of eighteenth-century oak and seats sixteen. It was here that I sat with a friend and was served by white-gloved butlers. The hands of those butlers, reaching discreetly around to serve and to remove my plates, seemed totally disembodied. They reminded me of the sconces Cocteau invented for the movie *Beauty and the Beast.* The candles were held by fingers of flesh that swayed and flickered in the wind.

When I long for privacy and quiet, I retreat behind the walls of my favorite study and read near the fire. The velvet curtains across the leaded glass windows in this room in my head are cinched as tightly as the belt of a woman's bathrobe. From this room, I occasionally hear the moans of a homesick ghost in the nearby tower, the ghost of a seventeenth-century blackamoor who was kidnapped from his hovel in Venice four hundred years ago.

I am someone who usually detests sentimental journeys, who never attends a high school reunion or reads a college newsletter. Yet there is very little in this home in my head that is new or modern. I seem to prefer the feel of magnificent wrecks furnished with memories as tattered as the faded silk drapes that hang in deserted salons. Perhaps this is because in those first trips to Europe it was precisely this intimacy, this proximity to the past, that created a whole new sense of the present for me. In traveling light at an age when fear kept others close to home but faith was far less fragile than it now appears, I was free to accumulate experience, the very thing my father once confessed was the only thing in life worth accumulating.

Seeing my father now strapped to his bed, attached to life by a thin green tube of oxygen, I realize that it has been years since this man had the power to move me, to make me laugh out loud or cry. It is only when I am about to take flight again, when I buckle myself in for a business trip to Hong Kong and fiddle with my seat-side phone, that I miss him. I miss him because I know that if my father were here on the runway with me, he too would wonder whatever happened not just to the romance of flight but of so many things in life that remain forever remote and faraway.

"i believe miss sewell is down here in my bushes."

TWELVE YEARS AGO, ON THE NIGHT I GAVE BIRTH TO Jack — to this son who has grown into a boy so remarkably gentle, we joke about him becoming a priest — a vital part of me remained so remote that I thought perhaps the anesthetic that had numbed me from the spine down had spread to my heart. While my husband tenderly held his first-born son, I lay on the delivery-room table, chatting with the doctor about his homeland, Yugoslavia, as he pumped out my placenta with his fist. Forget labor. Forget the maternal instinct and feeling connected to this child who had been in my womb or to the man who had planted the seed. It was Yugoslavia I felt connected to, this place where I'd once had a boyfriend and to which I had been so many times and knew so intimately that I felt like a native. This was a connection I could relate to.

It wasn't the fear of Jack's dependence on me as a mother that created such distance between us throughout the months I carried him or on the night I delivered him. People had always depended on me. The role of protector is what defined my power and gave me strength. No. It was my fear of becoming dependent upon Jack, of becoming too attached. In making this connection with Jack, in loving him, I would become vulnerable, helpless.

It is only now, in attempting to make some connection with my own parents, that I am able to see how much I owe my husband and my children. They are the ones who have taught me something about the joys of living not as if abandoned or in fear of being abandoned but with abandon. At times like this, I don't feel pity but sorrow for my parents. Because there is no place on earth that feels more remote to me now than that place in time when they first recognized the possibility of their own happiness — when they first saw the hope of a home in each other's eyes.

When Mother tells me that she still has the letters from Dad that date back to their early months of infatuation and dating, to the days when he was known as "Cully" and Mom as "Scoop" (an affectionate reference to her dreams of being a cub reporter), and that she's kept them hidden inside a wooden trunk at the bottom of the stairs for over forty years, I'm not so sure I want to open them. Prying into the past has become almost as frightening for me as I once assumed gazing into the future might be.

Why is it that my mother is suddenly so determined to travel back to that other moment in time? to that moment of revelation when I imagine they might have said to themselves, "Yes! Here is someone who finally understands me, who speaks my language"? Is it her way of declaring some kind of truce? of preparing herself for Dad's departure? Even as he continues to defy doctors and the odds against his surviving another month, I know that she is beginning to fear the impact of his death. We all are. Perhaps, now that he is so close to gone, Mom thinks the letters will bring him and whatever hopes of happiness she might have once had with him back to life. But I am in no such hurry to bring him back. I have grown accustomed to the absence of the man who once functioned as my father — a man whose invincible charm lay in the absolute effortlessness with which he seemed to inhabit it.

Of course, anyone who mistook that effortlessness for indifference, who underestimated my father and his extraordinary ability to see in the dark, to identify other people's hidden fears and frailties, did so at their own peril. Friends of my father have said they never once saw him lose his cool, that he was as self-possessed and as agile putting a Rolling Stone and an ambassador at ease as he was the Quakers at Clarks. Sober, he had a vitality, an energy, that made others around him in a room seem colorless, dull. But there was also the menacing side of my father, the side that like the unexpectedly rough, sandpapery skin of a shark leaves its prey lacerated and bleeding even before the moment of attack.

On the only night I ever dared to confront him about his drinking, on a night when I sat shivering and in tears on the living-room couch, stuttering my way through a speech I'd prepared that begged him to stop, he listened to me quietly, fired up a match with his thumb, lit a cigarette, and said: "Don't ever bring this up again, Brenda. Because what you do not understand, what you will never understand, is that I don't care. I have never cared."

My teeth were chattering as I got up to leave the room. So when I first pull the letters out and touch the flimsy folded envelopes postmarked Hanover, London, New York, and Rome, I feel as if I am touching a dead man. I have no desire to meet my father as a young man. Because it will hurt hearing his voice, seeing his handwriting, and remembering the days when a few of his well-chosen words still had the power to soothe and console me.

My father hasn't read a book in eighteen years. He can't decipher a newspaper caption. But as these letters remind me, it was definitely a mutual love and command of the English language that helped transform my parents into a couple. Even in his early twenties, my father sounds all grown-up, as if he were up at Dartmouth as some kind of amused observer of the "boys" around him. (It was the GI Bill that covered Dad's tuition. When he arrived at Dartmouth as a freshman, he had already spent two years building bridges with the Marines.) In one letter, he talks about how his fraternity brothers are "full of the usual piss and vinegar," then fills Mom in on their response to the draft. (The Korean War was just beginning.)

> *It's the first time in years these fatuous youths have been bothered by anything except a desire to go home. All in all, I find their panic quite stimulating. In fact, between the draft and the recalling of the reserves, the student body has been diminished for the better. Even the dean is busy for the first time in his uneventful life, writing letters to get the boys deferred for another year or two.*

There isn't a wasted word in Dad's writing. He was as terse and succinct, as ruthless an editor, when it came to putting thoughts on paper as he was in every other aspect of his life. But this must have been part of the attraction for Mother — how mature, how different, he seemed compared to other college kids. (Mother was a sophomore at Barat when they met.) Mom was a rebel, an outcast, and the fact that Dad was also an outsider — that he didn't belong to those elite and privileged ranks of Dartmouth preppies — made him even more alluring.

In another letter, there is a very brief mention of how he succeeds, for the first time in Dartmouth's history, in getting a Jewish friend into a fraternity. "There was no ultimatum, Mary. I simply suggested they accept his pledge or replace me as a brother. They accepted him." This boy never forgot my father's gesture. When David became a Hollywood producer years later, my parents would travel down to New York for premieres and parties at nightclubs like Shepherd's.

Between further chat about squash teams, snow, and the hunting season, Dad talks of "loneliness and my empty bed" and of money or the lack of it.

> *My financial situation is precarious to say the least, but I refuse to bow to the convictions of the adamant keeper of the bank. The airlines still cash my rubber checks, and I will be home to see you soon and often. I promise. I also have a position as a lackey in a local eating emporium which should enable me to save enough to have you up for the weekend.*

Home for Dad was a farmhouse in the town of Ridgebury, Connecticut. For Mother, anywhere more than five miles away from Ohehyahtah Place in Danbury may as well have been

Khartoum. "Ridgebury wasn't just the other side of the tracks; it was the boondocks. Nobody, but nobody, lived there." There was no Main Street, no hat factories, no rich families like hers and the Mallorys and the Lees, just farmers.

Mother had been educated at the Convent of the Sacred Heart. Her family vacationed in Sea Island and Bermuda. Dad had learned to read in a one-room schoolhouse. He'd sold goat's milk and trapped and shot squirrels and raccoons for their pelts to help support his widowed mother.

The night Dad finally invited Mom home to Ridgebury for supper, she met Dad's English mother, Marie, a heart-startlingly beautiful forty-three-year-old redhead who had danced onstage for European royalty, a woman whose house was filled with other glamorous émigrés like Hildegard, from the Ziegfeld Follies, and her sisters, Georgie and Rhodie, who performed in English musicals with the matinee idol Ivor Novello.

"At that first dinner, Rhodie and Georgie talked about their days dancing through the Blitz in London. They called the V2 rockets *doodlebugs.* During the war, my father had these maps of Europe in his study. They had pins all over them, marking the advance of the Allies. But I never knew there were real women like this, women who laughed at the Blitz and chatted about love affairs on yachts in strange towns with names like Portofino."

How enthralled, how bewitched, my mother must have been by this introduction to such an exotic and colorful world — a world so gloriously far away from the place she had come from. Even Dad's lack of money would have seemed romantic. Money for Mother had no value. It was a misery she would have been delighted to leave behind. "Your father had a mind that was clearer, sharper, than anyone's I have ever known," she says now. "There was nothing he couldn't do. We were crazy about each other."

But all of this happiness is ancient history now. As ancient as these letters I hold in my hands and the cast-iron bean slicer screwed onto the counter in our kitchen. It was Dad's wedding gift to Mom. "It looks like something left over from the Spanish Inquisition," Mom used to say with a giggle as she turned the crank that blanched the beans. But why, if my parents were once so happy, was there never any mention of a wedding day? There were no pictures at our house of the bride and groom, no white dress and veil packed in tissue in the attic. My parents never even celebrated an anniversary. Mom said she didn't approve of them. Anniversaries, like Secretary's and Mother's Day, were commercial events invented by "Hellmark."

For years, I assumed that their silence implied they were keeping yet another secret. I had fantasies about being illegitimate, about a shotgun marriage. But according to the yellowed newspaper clipping I found buried in the pages of one of Mother's favorite Dickens novels two years ago, the ceremony took place in May 1950 at an office of the justice of the peace in White River Junction. I was born eleven months later. It seems appropriate that my parents eloped — that they began their marriage on the run. In cynical moments I wonder if my grandfather's money might explain why my father decided to tie the knot. Long after Dad was en route to making his own *fortunatus ad um,* Grandpa was still giving him a fifty-dollar check and a piece of Mark Cross luggage every Christmas.

But Mom says they were a "golden couple" in those early years together. They lived in an apartment in Hanover while

Dad finished Dartmouth. After college and a year working for the shipping company W. R. Grace, he started a small clothing company called Fan Flair. Mom did the books for him.

This may have been the only time my mother experienced joy. Dad was her ticket out of her own backyard. He was her ally, the man who had rescued her from a battlefield of drunks and carried her into a new and sober homeland. How bizarre to think that this glamorous foreigner, this ally she'd married, would eventually become the drunken cripple she thought she'd buried, a man who would come back from the dead not just limping like her father in the same pair of Brooks Brothers pajamas but gasping for breath, belligerent and broke.

But unlike Grandpa Arnold, my father brilliantly assumed the role of rescuer and was gentle and compassionate when I was a child. I can see him running into the kitchen to save me from being electrocuted when my hands got frozen on the metal door of our short-circuited refrigerator. Dad shoved a wooden broomstick between me and the handle and wrenched me free. I was as blue as the shell of a hermit crab and shook for hours. I can see him diving off our dock at Lake Candlewood to rescue a city friend who was shrieking for help while drifting off into the distance on our overturned Sunfish. Dad climbed aboard and sailed them back to shore. And I can see him holding my mother, her head leaning against his shoulder, as he helped her up the stairs the night she heard one of her uncles had died. He'd burned to death, smoking a cigarette in bed.

For years, my mother boasted about my father, about how smart and funny he was. "Scathingly funny," she always said. In reading another letter that he wrote to her on a thin sheet of

Pan Am stationery while en route to London, I am shocked and delighted to discover that my father still has the power to make me laugh out loud.

Mary —
A fly has landed on my tray and justified the international concern. How does the plague pass from Delhi to Danbury? Now I see the answer — small, black, hairy, and comfortable, the fly is safe at 40,000 *feet, healthy and ready to pass on any American virus. Who knows where he will terminate his travels? On this, Pan Am flight* #1, *are all the cities of Europe south to the Asian Littoral and thence east to India and Bangkok. God knows his choice or virulence or selection of a site, but so passes the conglomerate infirmity from land to land.*

So far the trip is very exciting. The two people sharing my three abreast seat keep rubbing knuckles surreptitiously. They are serious, young, in love, and I would judge from Marion, Ohio, via Paul Stewart and Peck & Peck. A certain type so to speak.

Oh. And there was a bright flash and dull thud about 10 *minutes after takeoff that is yet to be explained. I believe it was lightning bouncing off the aircraft and either too commonplace to deserve comment or too frightening for the sightseeing captain to discuss. I assume it wasn't mechanical as we are still aloft. There is nothing to recommend this method of travelling except dispatch. Will telex upon arrival.*

Love, Bob

Dad had just begun his career at Clarks and was barely earning a living then. But those early years for Mother, of having so much less than she had as a McLachlan, were exhilarating. It wasn't she who dreamed of moving up in the world (or even of seeing it), of a bigger and better house, of fancy cars and clothes. These would become my father's dreams, his ambitions. Mother, of course, could afford to dismiss the value of money. She had always had it. Just as she could also afford to indulge in dreams of my father becoming a poet or a college professor. She didn't have to support us.

It's Marie's ramshackle old house in Ridgebury that occupies an almost hallowed space in Mother's recollections of those early years of marriage. Unlike Ohehyahtah, where the garden grew in neat little labeled rows, everything at Marie's, including the raspberry bushes, grew thick and wild and offered a perfect place for pretending to be an explorer like Stanley or Livingstone (Mother's favorites). I loved getting lost in that jungle. Armed with empty colanders and cooking pots, I'd head into the riot of bushes and come back to Marie's kitchen with my fingers stained red with juice and blood from thorns. In the winter, she'd send me down the street to Mrs. Elzer's to pick up quarts of fresh milk and heavy cream.

On weekends at Grandma's, I slept beneath a pile of pink silk eiderdowns on a bed under the eaves in Uncle Larry's old room. The house was freezing. Marie believed that heat was bad for one's health. There were no books in my grandmother's house. Grandma wasn't a reader. And no television, either. But when she tucked me into bed at night, I'd beg to hear the stories of her days as a girl when she sailed across the oceans on ships and danced for the Austrian archduke in Vienna. In the morning, she'd bundle me up in clothes she had warmed in the belly of a big black iron stove, and we'd eat crepes smothered in lemon juice and raspberry jam.

The State of Connecticut razed Grandma's house when they built Route 84 twenty-five years ago. All that is left of it now are the raspberry bushes my uncle transplanted for Marie when he built our back house. Larry worked very slowly after Dad hired him to build the house. First of all because it was a labor of love and he wanted to ensure that every luxurious detail suited the needs of his crippled mother. And second, because he was usually stoned out of his mind. The house took months to finish, and costs went through the roof. So did Dad. He was the one paying for it. Perhaps if he'd seen his own future as a cripple in that house, he would have complained less.

"God, how I loved Marie's," Mom says. "Those wonderful Christmases." I remember them too. After our mornings at Ohehyahtah Place, the cheerful anarchy at Marie's house came as a blessed relief. The tree, a towering blue spruce that Larry had cut down, dwarfed everything around it in the living room. It was hung with huge globes of blue-and-silver foil and necklaces of tiny white lights that were shrouded in cocoons of angel hair. Dad showed us how to pull the angel hair out of the package and wrap it around our fingers until it was shaped like a little sausage. We had to be careful of splinters. The angel hair was spun out of glass.

I haven't thought of that Christmas tree in over thirty years. But in seeing it now, I also see the wall that divided my grandmother's house. It's bizarre, how history seems to repeat itself in our family when it comes to building walls. The wall at Grandma's house was in her dressing room. It had a secret door. When you pushed it a certain way, it opened up, just like the door of the wardrobe in *The Lion, the Witch, and the Wardrobe.* It was only on Christmas Day, when the tenants were away, that we were allowed to enter the world that lay on the other side of that dressing-room wall.

It was a world of magnificently dressed foreign ladies, friends from the English theater, who came up from New York to Connecticut to celebrate an old-fashioned English Christmas. They sat with us at a long table covered in white damask, lit by silver candelabras. Between courses of black olives smothered in olive oil and onions, blanched green beans, Yorkshire pudding, and roast beef, they would take turns standing up and singing Noël Coward songs. (I still remember the words to "Don't Put Your Daughter on the Stage, Mrs. Worthington.")

At the end of the meal, Grandma made her final entrance, carrying a homemade plum pudding. There was something magical about that moment, not just because of the eerie blue light cast by the blue flames that licked the sides of the pudding but because it marked that moment in time when this world would literally disappear, when we would be forced to walk back through the secret dressing-room door into our everyday world.

Not that there was much about Marie or her sisters that seemed everyday to me as a child. They were marvelously mysterious and eccentric, these women who existed in a world so apart, that they needed no one else. Even their language, expressions like "spend a penny," "dogsbody," "hello, duckie," and "cheerio," made them exotic. I knew nothing then of the horrors, the lies, and the losses that, like the wall that divided Marie's house, lay just on the other side of their lightheartedness.

Only the stunningly erratic behavior of Dad's aunt, our English great-auntie Rhodie, hinted at darkness. Rhodie was a substitute baby-sitter. As devoted to us as she was dangerous, Rhodie traveled with a single possession — an ornate sterling silver framed mirror in which she said she could see the face of the only man she had ever loved. (His name was Dunstan.) It was Rhodie who replaced the notorious Mrs. Duryea when Mom and Dad took off on an occasional long-distance vacation.

Mrs. Duryea had bright-purple hair, lived in a trailer (we adored her trailer), and swore so obscenely, we had to respect her. "You ain't nothin' but a little shit!" was her favorite expression. That and "Git, g'won git!"

"Tell me what Mrs. Duryea says, kids. Please." Grandpa McLachlan laughed — more like wheezed — so hard when he heard our chorus of "little shit, little shit" from the backseat of his car, I was afraid he'd die trying to catch his breath. Then he'd show off his latest trick — steering with his one good foot.

Great-auntie Rhodie referred to her drinking as "a wee bit of tippling." One morning when Mom and Dad were away, she got so drunk she chased me up the back stairs with a carving knife. I had to lock myself in the bathroom until she slept it off. Rhodie's enthusiasm for the bottle was boundless. "I believe Miss Sewell is down here in my bushes," reported the matter-of-fact voice on the telephone. This was three days after I'd locked myself in the bathroom. It was our elderly neighbor, Mr. Hoyt. He had discovered Rhodie headfirst ("arse over teakettle") in his hydrangeas. She was singing ditties in Cockney rhyming slang. Her very brisk morning stroll had led directly to the liquor store two miles down the road. The return home was a bit less brisk. She polished off an entire quart of Four Roses before collapsing in the bushes.

Thankfully for Mr. Hoyt, Rhodie continued singing when

he gave her a hand and hoisted her up. She could have just as easily grabbed his gardening shears and stabbed him in the heart. Sober, Rhodie was a joy. Drunk, she turned into Bette Davis in *What Ever Happened to Baby Jane?* After repeatedly hitting Marie over the head with a cane, she moved back from their house in Del Ray Beach, Florida, to live with us permanently.

One of four sisters, Rhodie was eight when she found her father, my great-grandfather, dead in the family garden shed in Surrey. A professional acrobat and an alcoholic, he'd stuck himself in the neck with a pair of hedge clippers. This was shortly after falling off the top of a human pyramid at a carnival outside Liverpool. "Of course, he did the right thing," Rhodie's nephew, Deansy, told me while nibbling on a salmon steak, after Rhodie died.

"Forgive me, Deansy," I interrupted, "but how do you figure sticking a hedge clipper in your neck is the right thing?"

"Well, the accident left him soft in the head, dear. He would have been a burden to his family." I had never heard anything quite so cruel or casual. Or had I?

It was then I remembered my father's reaction when the phone rang one Sunday afternoon years ago and Rachel picked it up.

"Hello, is Bobby there?" a woman asked.

"Can I tell him who's calling?"

"Tell him it's Jackie." LONG PAUSE. "His sister."

Rachel thought it was a joke. We all did. We'd never heard of a sister. Dad's "explanation" was out of Ripley's Believe It or Not! The forceps used to help deliver Jackie had damaged her brain at birth. "She wasn't very bright," Dad said. "So we didn't see each other much."

It was my mother who filled in the blanks. Unable to accept the fact that her daughter was less than perfect, Dad's mother and her sons cut Jackie dead. None of her pathetic cries for attention — her unruliness at school, her drinking, her sleeping around at the age of thirteen — made the slightest difference. They just pretended she wasn't there. This went on right up to the day she ran away from home at sixteen. Until the phone rang that Sunday afternoon, forty-five years later, no one had ever once mentioned her name.

These days, shrinks would probably attribute such behavior to some kind of severe "detachment disorder." Like the day Rhodie skinned and cooked my pet rabbit, Oscar, after he froze to death in his pen outdoors. It was Dad who recognized the scent of rabbit simmering on the stove and stopped Oscar from arriving at the table. "It's the rationing," he told us. "Rhodie remembers the rationing during the war." I figured it was just part of being English. All their emotions, like the messages we hurled out to sea on our summers up in Maine, were corked into a bottle. A Scotch bottle.

When that bottle of Dewar's was opened, the side of my father that seemed so reassuringly sane compared to Mother gave way to a quiet seething, to a stillness that sent us all scurrying for cover. The abruptness of that shift from one mood to another, from gentleness to rage, from compassion to cruelty, was like the strange trick the sky does when you fly across the North Atlantic. There was this quick switch from the brightness of day into night and back again.

When the fury hit and darkness descended, there were no fiery balls in the sky. No warnings. But the explosions sent off a series of rippling tremors. The ground seemed to shudder beneath our feet and cave in on itself, leaving us with no one but each other to hold on to. I witnessed only two of my father's explosions. The first was after an argument with Mother. It wasn't her screaming that had us shaking at the top of the banister. It was his silence. That and the terrible sounds of a wooden chair being ever so slowly and methodically broken into teensy-eensy bits with his bare hands. The implication was obvious. He was breaking every bone in her body. "Save it and use it as kindling," he nonchalantly said, pointing to the tidy pile of splintered remains that lay at her feet.

The second time, years later, I was peering over Mom's shoulder in the den as she opened a beautiful green velvet box. Next thing I knew, a glittering blur of metal and stone went flying across the room. It hit my father in the face. "Come with me, Mary," Dad said in a voice so flat, I shivered. "I want to show you something." As they headed out to the garage, I ran upstairs and hid. It wouldn't have surprised me if he'd killed my mother. What he did instead was gently place his gift, this three-thousand-dollar diamond wristwatch, in the mouth of a vise on his tool bench and turn the screws until nothing was left of it but bits of shattered springs and crystal.

It was the containment of rage, the silence, and the deliberateness of his every gesture and word that made us tiptoe around my father. He was so exquisitely controlled, even when he was out of control. Rachel still remembers her terror the day she brought home a report card at age twelve. She had two B's. The rest were A's. "So, darling," Dad said with a wicked grin, "how does it feel to be falling into the abyss of mediocrity?" Being mediocre for Dad was no different than being mongoloid. It meant you were less than perfect. Defective. Like Jackie. "Addlepated troglodyte," "nonstarter," and "feckless fop" were other choice phrases used to define and dismiss those who didn't measure up to Dad's exacting standards of perfection. It's unspeakably ironic that my father ended up so far from perfect himself, not just addlepated but "soft in the head" like his grandfather, his sister Jackie, and his own mother.

But most of my father's life seems to have been shrouded in the same fuzzy, dim light I associate with those cocoons of angel hair we placed on the Christmas tree. Loss never loosened his tongue the way it did my mother's. Even before the stroke deprived him of most of his speech, Dad never spoke of his childhood or his early years with his mother, Marie. It was as if he had simply deleted this huge chunk of experience from his memory. Nothing sparked a connection, not even when he decided to name our son, Jack. (Jack was the name of my father's father, the man who died when Dad was six.)

I wonder, for instance, if Dad ever realized that both he and his mother had lost their fathers at the same age? Was it the impact of this loss at the age of six that somehow explained their shared silence, their detachment? What else didn't I know about Marie, about this woman who for forty-five years had refused to mention the name of her daughter but who never seemed to need consoling, a woman who, even after her own stroke, even after her sister had attacked her with a wooden cane, continued to hold her head high, to weed and water her plants with one good hand while cheering me on as I danced naked through the sprinklers on our front lawn as a teenager?

"bend, you fool!"

As I plump the pillows behind my mother's head, after serving her soup, crackers, and her small half glass of cold tap water with no ice, she seems to sink deeper and deeper into the pleasures of recalling her husband's past. Unlike the sharp-edged bitterness that accompanied her talks of the McLachlans, there is a certain pride and wistfulness, even admiration, in her memories of the Cullertons. It's been five months since we first began these conversations. When I sit down in New York to write about them, I feel as if I am being pulled forward, not pushed from behind, by something. It's odd but captivating, this sensation of being pulled, not pushed.

"Your grandfather Jack Cullerton was a real Stage Door Johnny," Mom tells me. She's finished the soup, and her eyes are closed. I'm sitting in her pink chintz armchair, discreetly trying to inch the window open. "It's painted shut," she says, opening one eye. "It's been that way since 1980. Now listen to me. Jack was the fire commissioner of Chicago in the 1930s. The Cullertons had been part of the political machine down there for donkey's years." I immediately picture Jack as a close friend of Al Capone and the Mob. He had to have been connected. No one with power and influence in 1930s Chicago survived without connections. "Jack fell in love with your grandmother after watching her perform in an English musical revue. She was nineteen years old."

Grandma's mother had put Marie and three of her sisters on the stage not long after her husband's suicide. By her midteens, Marie was starring in shows that had taken her "across the pond" to the States and as far away as Alexandria and Cairo. She had seen the world. But her life "on the boards" was as strictly regimented as a young soldier's. Like her sisters Georgie, Rhodie, and Edith, Marie had trained with the famous La Loïe Fuller in London. La Loïe was a friend of Marie's fourth and oldest sister, Cissie, whom Noël Coward talks about at great length in his 1937 autobiography, *Present Indicative*.

Mom met Cissie when she sailed over to England in the early seventies. "It was a pilgrimage for me, after all the years of hearing Rhodie's stories. Cissie was as tough as nails, living alone in a bed-sit in Shepherd's Bush. We had tea, and she talked about her front-row seats at the opening night of *Bitter Sweet* on Broadway. Noël had paid her passage over as a thank-you for all her hard work. He adored her. But Cissie hated Jack."

Cissie's plan was to turn Marie into a star as bright as Gertie Lawrence or Billie Burke. With the contacts she had, she probably could have done it. Marie eloped instead. Her husband was fifty-three. She was nineteen and already a survivor.

But it was the eagle-eyed supervision, not the tender loving care of women like La Loïe and her sister Cissie, that had made her so. She was a girl who literally had to sing for her supper. With Jack, there would be no more grueling rehearsals or auditions, no more fears of rejection or packing and unpacking of steamer trunks or lonely nights in distant cities.

Until the day her fairy tale came to its tragic end eight years later, Marie lived like one of those heirs of an Ottoman sultan in a golden cage. Mom says that she had a fancy house in Evanston complete with Oriental rugs, servants, silver, and a chauffeur-driven Pierce Arrow. As isolated in her suburban palace as these ill-fated princes were in their golden cages, with only her sisters and small children for company (who knew as little about the world outside their doors as the deaf-mutes who served the Sultan's brothers), Marie would arrive for an afternoon vigil at her husband's deathbed only to find him surrounded by two ex-wives and a tribe of stepchildren she had never even known existed.

"She was young and naive, you see, and Jack had taken such beautiful care of her until the end. He was the father she never had." But exactly like my own father, who squandered away his millions and left his family virtually bankrupt before his stroke, Jack also left his wife with a mountain of debts so high that everything from the house to the Pierce Arrow had to be sold. It was then her brother Archer stepped in to rescue her. Archer had set up a business in Australia and invited Marie and the children to join him as soon as they could get away. Three weeks before they were to set sail, Archer put a bullet in his head. "It was Rhodie who told me about Archer. Your grandmother never mentioned it. It was too painful."

One of my favorite but forbidden pleasures as a kid was sneaking into the barn behind Grandma's house and opening her fabulous leather steamer trunks. The trunks were covered with stickers from all the great old ships and hotels. Inside were stacks of playbills and Grandma's costumes — neatly folded pastel silk and satin dresses with lace fans and slippers to match. These were the moth-eaten dreams of fame that Marie's marriage to Jack Cullerton had forever annulled. They burned to the ground together with everything else that Grandma had managed to save from the financial and emotional wreckage of her past.

This is just some of the baggage my father carried throughout our childhood and his marriage. Its weight made him as rigid and unyielding as the tree in his favorite old *New Yorker* cartoon. As funny as it was prophetic, the cartoon still hangs in his living room. "Bend, you fool!" says the caption beneath a picture of four trees. A gale-force wind is blowing, and three of the trees are bent over double. The fourth stands alone, ramrod-straight, proudly defying the very thing that is about to snap it in two.

It comes as no surprise that a stroke finally paralyzed my father's stiff upper lip. Or that all that is left to him are obscenities — the expressions of a primal rage, a railing against his fate. What a hideous fate for a man who prided himself on being so precise, on perfection. Like the nursery rhymes we sang with him in rehab, these fits of rage are a reminder that in the end there isn't much that separates the child from the grown-up.

Like Mom, Dad too grew up in a void. A fearful void created by a mother who had been betrayed, abandoned by her father, her mother, her husband, her brothers. Even the birth of an imperfect daughter may have been seen as a kind of betrayal. A stranger to all but desertion and that impending sense and fear of loss, it seems inevitable that Marie should have turned her sons into drifters. Drifters who in turn would betray, through rage and rejection, not just the possibility of their own feelings and those who tried to love them but their own futures.

Sometimes I wish Dad had just screamed like Mother or hit or spanked us. But my father never snapped at or physically hurt any of us as kids. He vacuumed or chipped paint instead. Nevertheless, we were so accustomed to the precariousness of those fundamental things that most children take for granted — guidance, acceptance, an illusion of safety — that we acquired the same keen instincts that allow animals to survive in the wild. As a result, most pets were more housebroken, more domesticated, than we were.

"Little savages! You oughta live in cages!" This is how one friend of my parents described us before escaping in his car when we were young. A photographer who eventually hanged himself in his garage had been hired to do a portrait of us while Mom and Dad were away on vacation. For three solid hours, we sabotaged every shot, sticking out our tongues and giving him the finger the instant he clicked the shutter.

"Pig! Pig!" I'd howl at Mom as she chased me around the couch. "I'm going to tell your father. I'm writing this one down," she'd bellow back. When Dad was gone (more and more often), she'd pull out her black book. It was the only threat that worked. Dad scared the hell out of us. Mother was all bark. He was the bite.

I paid no attention to Mom's bellowing. She did it all the time. Her hysteria, her screaming, wasn't just a sign of her lack of control. It was an excuse for relinquishing it. Her powerlessness forced others into doing precisely as she wished. Not me, though. Once I had mastered the art of silence, Mother was terrified of me.

My silence may have been a form of self-preservation. Mom was voracious in her neediness and her divalike display of extreme emotions like anger and despair. But there was no quieting her harrowing cries of loss and betrayal, no way to comfort her. This ghetto of grief, her despair . . . it was all part of the drama, the pain, and the conspiracy of suffering that had created her identity.

My distance from my mother certainly helped forge an alliance with my father, an alliance reinforced by my own determination to compensate for Mother's failure to perform or to meet anyone's expectations but her own. Unlike her, I would be perfect: a perfect daughter, a perfect student, a perfect friend. This was the only way to make myself visible; to be loved. It's only now that I recognize perfection as yet another hellish form of precariousness.

If only I had known that Mother's screaming and Dad's silence were symptoms of a similar, shared despair. The despair of detachment, of isolation. This is what bound them so inextricably together and also kept them apart. They were like hostages held captive by a string of barbed wire, and their mutual struggles to free themselves — to risk traveling across that vast and unknown space that separates one human being from another — only seemed to dig the wire in deeper, to enrage them.

How could my mother, a woman who confused her need for recognition with the act of making a spectacle of herself, even begin to relate to my father, a man for whom appearances and a perfect performance would matter almost as much as they had for his mother back in her days of rehearsals and auditions? How could a woman who had never left her past behind, who lived only to remember the Alamo, love a man who had no past and who preferred only to forget? Better to pretend the other wasn't there — to build a wall, to keep moving.

There is one final letter in Mother's collection. It's postmarked 1974 and was written by my father after his session with John Brooke. In that letter (which I sneak off and read privately in my room), my father's words seem to have worn as thin as his temper and his tolerance of Mother. Even the language that once served as a common bond now only serves to remind me of the gulf that had always separated them.

There is no use of *dear* in his preface, just the clipped and succinct use of his wife's first name:

> *Mary:*
> *I had an interesting meeting this morning with Dr. Brooke. In summarizing his assessment of me on the issue of hostilities, deep-seated or otherwise, his feeling is that they simply do not exist as a characteristic of my personality. What does exist and is readily confused with hostility is anxiety.*
>
> *This anxiety apparently consumes huge amounts of otherwise useful energy just to keep under control. The primary contributing factor to this tension is a technique I have used for years, probably since childhood, for dealing with stress situations. Unlike yourself, Mary, I am not nor will I ever be a successful screamer. Silence is my voice. I am one who prefers to avoid or slip around issues in the interest of tranquility or safety . . . neither of which has ever been your priority. . . .*
>
> *He also seems to feel that much of my poor behavior and*

anxiety or stress at home is due to the fact that me and others like me in this world are at the very bottom of your status ladder. If you were to define the qualities in a man you liked best, I wouldn't have many at the top. And if you were also asked to pick the occupations you thought most worthy, business would be at the bottom, too. . . .

Although the ink has faded and the tissue-thin blue letter paper is crackled with age, the last two sentences, this simple, childlike plea on the part of my father to be recognized by his wife for his achievements, cry out to me as loudly as they cried out on the day they were written. It wasn't just the drinking, the departures, or even Mother's depressions that doomed their marriage. It was disappointment. Mother's disappointment in her husband's less-than-cerebral ambitions and her frustration, her loneliness, when faced with his absence. And my father's disappointment in a wife who couldn't be with him to share his triumphs.

There is nothing more debilitating, more damaging, to a relationship than disappointment, than the suspicion that one has failed the person one loves. Unfortunately, the danger of disappointing my father lay not in inciting his rage but in being cut off. Disappointing him meant you disappeared. You were dead and forgotten like his "addlepated" sister, Jackie; his hapless, troubled son, Geoff; his "irresponsible" brother, Larry; and his own wife.

"please, don't tell me. i don't want to know."

The miraculous thing about the month of May in a place where nothing is ever weed-whacked, trimmed back, pruned, or mowed, is how the wild, luxuriant growth hides every defect and flaw. The forsythia has transformed the backyard into a billowing blaze of yellow light. Even the grass has grown so high down near the barn that the carcasses of our old cars are covered up. For one brief hallucinatory moment as I push Nora on the big rubber tire that hangs from a branch of our maple tree, I almost believe that this could be a house like any other.

But Geoff says that Mother is now making fifteen phone calls a day to the back house. Sometimes I think Mother is possessed by her husband. Possessed in the ways her inability to move or to read, her belligerence, and her lapses into obscenity have begun to mirror his own. Despite the walls, the distance, the warring, my mother has somehow slipped into my father's skin and become him.

She can't stand being alone, even for the amount of time it takes Pearlie to complete another ridiculous chore. Pearlie is from Queens and replaces Bernice on weekends. "Mom's had Pearlie polish the silver under the bed three times since Friday," Geoff tells me on the phone. "What do you think she's planning, the Boston Tea Party? Please come up here and help. I'm going insane."

My last visit up was two weeks ago when I came to meet Pearlie. "Traveling light, huh, Pearlie?" I'd said, on the Saturday morning she stepped into Mother's kitchen carrying nothing but a small bag and a Gideon Bible.

"Don't need to carry nothin' with me, mon, but the good Lord's word." Pearlie's English is pure Jamaica. The night she tried to tempt Mother into eating her *gunga,* I thought she said *ganga.* "You can't do this," I whispered. "Mother's high enough as it is."

"This id'in *ganga,* mon. It's *gunga.* Peas. Peas and rice."

When she's not cooking or "talking in tongues," as Mom says, with her husband on the phone, she's praying.

This time, Pearlie and Geoff are in Dad's laundry room when I come in to give my father a hug.

"You got's to talk wid your mother, Geoffrey," says Pearlie. She's pulling what's left of a French pink cotton nightgown out of the dryer. "Big holes in everyting, mon. She makin' me do da laundry with Lysol and ammonia."

"Shit," says Geoff.

"And she trowin' tings at me. Tootbrushes and glasses."

While Geoff heads over to talk to Mom, I try talking with Dad. They've upped his dosage of Ativan. He's lost all concept of time and is awake all night, shouting for everything from his winter coat to cold bottles of Yoo-Hoo. "Bastard!" he whispers as I rearrange the mask over his face. Why am I always yawning in here? When I collapse on the blue-and-white-striped couch, I have to fight to keep my eyes open. *Say something, Brenda. Say something!* I shout to myself. "Gotta go!" I finally whisper, giving him a quick kiss. "Mom hasn't seen me yet."

"Watch your toes in there," Geoff says in a stage whisper as he points to Mom's bedroom door. "She's hidden all the carving knives behind the radiator and under the bed with the silver."

"Oh my God!"

"I said to her, 'Hey, Ma, do me a favor, will you? Stop walking around with sharp pointed objects. You might fall and hurt yourself.'

"'I'm afraid, Geoff.'

"'Afraid of what?' I said. 'Being filleted in your bed? Cause that's what I'm going to do to you if you keep pushing Pearlie around.'"

If it were any woman but my mother stumbling around with a fistful of carving knives, wheedling, whining, and rattling her walker, I'd probably believe the doctors who say she is manifesting symptoms of senile dementia or Alzheimer's. I think it's the remnants of rage and resistance. This is what has given her these new, unexpected bursts of energy. Even her appetite has improved. She's gained five pounds in the past two weeks, and she's talking about driving again.

I know I should be elated, relieved at what may be signs of my mother's recovery. But the thought of her delayed departure fills me with guilt. I'm tired of living with death threats, of gritting my teeth and gearing up for nothing but aborted take-offs. There's a part of me that would like to murder both my parents right now. Sickness and pain often make people selfish. But neither of my parents ever make requests. They demand. They're terrorists. And there's no negotiating with terrorists.

The anger at my father comes out in ways as suppressed as Mrs. DiMarco's tiny sneezes. Like when I steal his favorite ash-tray. "Even if he's too far gone to notice, that's not the point," says my brother. "It's his. It belongs to him." Geoff is right. Like the heavy old oak mail tray from the Hibernian in Dublin, the ashtray from the Hassler is an object that anchors my father's own memories of the far away in place.

Stealing it may have been a way of trying to hurt him, of saying "Fuck you," like Mother did with her parents' silver. It may also have been a way of trying to get closer to him, to the times when I loved and looked up to him. For years, I consid-ered myself lucky. The only relationship my brother and sister seem to have had with my father was through the lists he left behind on yellow legal pads. *Mow the lawn; cut your hair; do your homework*. But unlike me, my brother and sister rebelled. In refusing to perform, they became Mother's allies. I carried the flag for my father like some crusader fighting against the infidels. Always the first to blame my mother for his falls from grace and to forgive his slips into the viciousness of failure.

If he drank, it was because Mother drove him to it. "A fucking funny farm, that's what it is," he'd say, after a few stiff drinks in a hotel lobby. "She's turned my house into a fucking funny farm." If he had other women, gorgeous women who seemed to dote on him and who took care of him, it was be-cause Mother couldn't or wouldn't take care of him. I was the only one in the family who took care of my father, the only one who understood that he was a man one had to handle with great care, if only for fear of what carelessness might unleash.

The night my father had his stroke, I had a premonition. I dreamed I was falling in an elevator. When it crashed, I was alive but couldn't speak or move. I could hear people calling my name when Mother's phone call woke me up. "Your father's in Danbury Hospital," she curtly announced. "He's had a very bad stroke."

When he picked up the phone at the lake the night before, all Mom heard was groans. She and a friend, Louis Rotello, drove up to meet the ambulance. Dad was sprawled out naked on the living-room couch, his whole body hideously cut up and bruised.

Staring at the man who lay moaning in gibberish on his clean hospital bed, I wanted to run. I wanted to run away just as fast as my legs would carry me. Instead I watched my mother nervously eyeing the exit signs as she paced the hallway. How could a woman who could barely do a load of laundry, vacuum, change a sheet, or cook begin to handle the life of an invalid, an invalid from whom she had separated herself not just emotionally but with a three-foot soundproofed wall more than fifteen years before?

For the next eleven years, Dad lived in his apartment at Gramercy Park, where a buxom blond nurse named Dorothy Dolliver, his friend Ronald Mullins, and my sister and I took care of him. I've blocked out most of those years: the trudging down the green linoleum corridors at Rusk, where Dad went for his rehabs; the shopping at Brooks Brothers for his pajamas, corduroy pants, and pinstriped shirts; the Sunday brunches at the Gramercy Park Hotel; and the endless juggling of the needs of a family for whom I had assumed this bizarre and previously unheard-of role as "conservator."

These were times of radical extremes in my own personal life and in the lives of my brother, sister, and mother. I had fallen in love and was living with Richard in New York. My brother was in his own rehab, recovering from cocaine addiction, while his wife struggled to care for their firstborn son, and my sister had one foot in and one foot out of a relationship with the man she would eventually decide to marry. Then there were financial decisions, crucial decisions on which the entire future of my parents would depend.

Throughout those eleven years of one crisis after another, I had no adults to turn to for advice or comfort. I stood as straight as I knew how and tried to keep some kind of balance. I relied on Richard and my instincts and made as many good decisions as truly terrible ones.

But just like Mom, who was never able to forgive her own mother for her helplessness, for not standing up to Arnold down in that basement and fighting back when he hit her with his fists, I couldn't forgive my mother, either. She had abandoned us. Yet again. In all those years, I seemed to feel empathy for everyone's helplessness but hers. And of course, my own. I couldn't afford to be helpless or lose my head. Not when everyone else was doing it for me.

The only moments when I lost my footing with Dad were when the lines between my duties as a daughter and those that defined the roles of doctor or wife became blurred. Listening to my father's therapists talk to me about his depression and frustrations was no problem. "Sharing" information about his physical needs and trying to act casual when they recommended I hire a sexual surrogate made me cringe.

I remember fighting the infantile urge to put my hands over my ears and hum while they talked. This forced intimacy with the man whose sperm had conceived me felt like incest or rape, a violation of the boundaries that kept father and daughter safely apart. When my father rubbed his hands together after his first session with the surrogate, winking and grinning, I begged him, "No. Please, don't tell me. I don't want to know." Just as I hadn't told anyone about that afternoon with Tommy on the mountain, I never told anyone about the surrogate. I paid the bills and kept the knowledge of those visits to a cold and sterile office where my father went through the motions of making love, a dirty secret from everyone.

This wasn't the first time I was keeping my father's other women a secret, of course. But there was something revolting to me about the idea, even about the term *sexual surrogate*. What did these women wear? I wondered. Nurses uniforms? Pantsuits and pumps? Unlike love affairs or high-class call girls and escort services, this therapy seemed utterly bereft of illusions or passion. It also made my father seem like a child, and to pay for a child to have sex made me feel sordid.

To wield this power of life and death over my own father, to control his money, even his sex life, and to keep his faithlessness a secret from his wife, damaged me. It placed me in a position of omnipotence, where protecting him seemed to demand that I betray my mother — something I am now ashamed to admit I did with few, if any, regrets.

Distance, again, became the key to my own survival. Only when I occasionally woke up at night in a cold sweat and my husband and children were sleeping did I permit myself to slip into my father's skin and relive the horror of that moment when he lay helpless on the couch. This is when I wept. How long had he been there? Was he cold? What did it feel like to be wordless? unable to move? alone? Was it someone he knew who had come into his house and kicked and punched him senseless?

Physical violence didn't happen to men who wore tweed sport coats, cashmere sweaters, and corduroys, and who drove BMWs. It happened to people I visited in faraway places like Africa and Guadeloupe. There, on the night of a full moon, a friend named Florent shared a supper of p'tit punch and fresh-caught grilled swordfish along with skin-prickling tales of malevolent humans he knew who had come back from the dead in the shape of dogs to hunt children's souls, of neighbors who could fly, and girls possessed who woke up with frogs and gramophones in their stomachs.

It was the second time I had a premonition, a nightmare about violence, that I finally began to see the disasters in my parents' lives not as inexplicable bad luck or haphazard coincidence but as a series of connections as intricately knit as the narrow and circuitous alleys in the Syrian souk where that second nightmare sprang to life.

I still have no idea why, in 1996, I chose Syria as a romantic getaway when my husband is a Jew. I knew I needed to feel the shock of what for me is always new — the unimaginably old. I needed to fall off the map, to get lost. The first night Richard and I went out in Damascus and Richard showed our taxi driver a map with our destination neatly circled on it, the taxi driver turned the map upside down. He squinted at it sideways. He laughed. It was meaningless to him. He had never seen a map.

But for the first three weeks we were in Syria, my husband encountered more kindness than anywhere else he could remember. There was Mr. Fix-It, the Palestinian engineer who begged us to phone him when we arrived at the bus station in the city of Homs and who came to pick us up and take us home for dinner. And Ali, the shoemaker who, when he caught us peeking through the doors of a seventeenth-century madrasah, introduced us to his students, then walked us back to his cubbyhole of a shoe store in a nearby courtyard. "English is my bobby," he said, meaning *hobby,* while serving endless pots of sweet tea. There was also the Hashemite named Turquis. Turquis could trace back his own roots, the roots of his tribe, as well as those of four other Middle Eastern heads of state, five generations. After driving us into the old town in Damascus, he sat us down in a restaurant, where we ate and talked until three o'clock in the morning.

This is what I remember most — this longing on the part of everyone we met to talk. And the men, always the men, Christians and Muslims, who trudged or drove miles out of their way to deliver us to our destinations, who opened up the doors of their hovels, tents, and palaces. All of them strangers. Honored to assuage our insatiable appetite for the unfamiliar, the unknown. "You are welcome here." It wasn't a trite expression. It was serious and true.

It was the second night of our stay at the Hotel Baron in Aleppo when I had the dream. The Baron was on its last legs. A symbol of empires as rickety as the idea of royalty itself, the hotel still advertised morning calls and English teas in its flimsy, onionskin-thin brochure. "Leave your breakfast order with the night porter," it suggested. The night porter was a thug in a shiny suit who scared the hell out of even the Russians at the hotel.

Here in the hotel's deserted restaurant, where T. E. Lawrence had probably devoured the same breakfast of cheese and olives, bread and yogurt, I told Richard I had dreamed of sitting on a dirt floor, cradling his bleeding head in my lap. He had dreamed of directing a movie. A gaffer was hit on the head by a falling beam. Desperate calls to 911 went unanswered as the man went into seizures.

Three hours later, we met a freckled, curly-haired tout outside a mosque in the souk. His name was Idris. "I have treasures for the lady," Idris promised, "Very old lapis bracelet. Not made yesterday, I assure you, madam." Taking hold of my elbow, he led us through a labyrinth of alleyways and shops. Dizzy with the scent of cardamom, cloves, saffron, and dry roses and the stink of grease and sweat, I was enraptured. Bare bulbs flickered and plunged us into split seconds of primordial darkness before candles and kerosene lamps shed a magic light on shelves of gold, silk, striped cottons, and silver.

I was in a tiny stall trying on Bedouin bridal shawls when I heard the screams. Idris was standing in the alley somewhere behind me. The silver threads of the shawl had unraveled and were caught in my fingernails. When I turned around to look, I saw four men hitting him over the head with the heavy iron poles used to roll up shutters in the souk. I could hear the crunch of metal smashing into bone and the grunts of effort as the men swung their poles high up into the air and then down onto his skull. "You see? You see?" Idris howled. He was on his knees, staring at me. See what? Too much blood, just like in my dream, all over his face and his blue shirt. His hands were flying as he tried to shield himself from the blows. When the men closed in on him and his shrieks faded into whimpers, Richard grabbed my hand and we ran.

The souk, which until moments ago had enthralled me, now seemed to asphyxiate every feeling but fear. A giddy, gut fear that made it hard to breathe. Pushing our way through a crowd that inched its way forward, we were trapped by burros laden with burlap sacks, black-shrouded women, and Bedu herding sheep. When we escaped into the sunlight, everything had changed.

Why? Why? I kept asking Richard. It couldn't have been over a commission. Had Idris gone to a hospital? Was he dead? Of course, he was dead. If only we had walked a second slower or faster, we would have missed him. Never met. Sitting drowsily in a cracked leather chair in the bar at the Baron, I realized these were stupid questions. Because here, unlike at home, there were no questions. Only faith. "There is no other God but God. And Muhammad is the prophet of God." Here, everything was "written" and exactly as God willed it. *"Inchallah."*

The vision of Idris, bleeding and swallowed in a mob of enraged men, traveled with us everywhere we went in Syria and also seemed to trigger new questions about my father. Maybe Dad hadn't been just a helpless victim that night they found him on the couch, naked and beaten. Maybe he wasn't innocent after all. Over the years, my nerves had become numbed by the sight of so much wreckage around me at home. Suddenly, Idris and his screams, that strange cry, "You see? You see?" had awoken them. What did I see? Or not see? What was it that I had refused to look at in all my years of disappearing and playing hide-and-seek?

On our last weekend in Syria, Richard and I visited the ancient city of Palmyra. The city itself is still miraculously preserved, so intact it seems to rise from its oasis like an Atlantis stranded in the sands. For two days we saw almost no one but Bedu. They lived in the ruins in summer tents that were shaped like long black caterpillars and approached us only to cadge cigarettes or herd their sheep out of our way.

At the end of our second day in Palmyra, a young British couple invited us to share a beer. Sitting at a table made from a fragment of a two-thousand-year-old marble column, we ate dates and exchanged the usual small talk between travelers about the trip, other places we'd been, and home.

"So where in England are you from?" asked Richard.

"Cambridge," said Adam. "But we're moving to the States right after our vacation."

"Really? Where to? New York? LA?"

"No one's ever heard of this town we're going to," said his wife, Alex, with a sigh. "It's called Ridgefield. It's in Connecticut."

"You've got to be kidding," I spluttered, spilling half a bottle of beer into my lap.

How slim were the odds of meeting two total strangers in the middle of a Syrian desert who were moving to Ridgefield? "Whoever said all roads lead to Rome was a liar," Richard said with a chuckle as we slid beneath the sheets at the Hotel Zenobia. "For you, they only seem to lead home."

It was when I returned home from Syria that I decided to write about my family. And this is when I began to see the history of violence buried beneath the rubble in my own backyard. At first, that history came alive only in brief, strobelike glimpses: the alcoholism, our car crashes, my cousin's drug overdose, those terrifying spasms of rage that had my father breaking chairs not bones. Then I saw him bruised and beaten on his hospital bed. Now, after five months of listening to my mother, I also see my great-grandfather sticking a pair of hedge clippers in his neck, Archer shooting a bullet through his brain, Rhodie bashing her sister over the head with a wooden cane and chasing me upstairs with a carving knife. I see fistfights, my grandmother's broken, bleeding nose, and my mother flying all over the friendly skies with a drunk in the cockpit.

Could those mortal fears of the hydrogen bomb that I had as a child, like my fascination for the underground shelters our neighbors built into basements and furnished with homemade bunk beds and wooden tables, have been some sort of internalization of that rage and violence? For our family, of course, there was no need for shelters. Not because my parents knew how useless they would be in the face of a real attack, but because it was the enemy within, it was self-annihilation, that would destroy us all. This is why my family had no sense of the future, why my mother lived every day as if it were yesterday and my father as if there were no tomorrow.

But whether self-inflicted or inflicted by another, I no longer believe that there is any such thing as a small or inconsequential act of violence or rage. Just as there are no random acts of violence. Because all such acts begin and end with the wounded. What does seem to be random, truly arbitrary, is whatever it is that determines who recovers from those wounds. Why do some rely only on suffering for a sense of their own significance while others don't? Is it in the genes, something "written" as destiny? Is the capacity to be comforted something we are born with or that we acquire?

Unlike my mother and father, I do seem to have found a path out of the wreckage. I live in a loft where there are no walls. The spaces my husband and I have carved from this old Village loft are as inspired by my memories of castles as they are of convent cells and of the berths and bunks where I first felt secure aboard ships and trains. There are old velvet curtains, crystal chandeliers, Oriental carpets, and striped poles and windows like the churches in Moscow and St. Petersburg. I've painted the walls in great sweeps of color: bright turquoise, yellow, tangerine, and pink. The flamboyance, the fearlessness, here in my house proves, at least to my children, that I am more than a mere ghost.

I even have a shrine, or the shell of a shrine. It's from Bolivia. I've stapled up a fragment of frayed peach silk inside. The silk is French, hand-embroidered in the eighteenth century with flowers and crowns and golden sequins. The shrine is filled with souvenirs from both the far away and the here and now. There's a lady's hand, a door knocker, from Syria. A wiggly picture of an old liner, the *France*. A jeweled snake head from a Burmese dagger. There are also photographs of Richard, Jack, and Nora, and a tiny book of snapshots a friend made as a gift after a vacation on the island of Vieques.

Maybe this shrine is a symbol of the self that has finally begun to emerge from its life as a sleeper, a life in hiding as a professional ghostwriter, a translator, a confidante, and a confessor. My struggle now to get out from beneath other people's skins and to be understood seems selfish. I realize that when sleepers are awoken, they often betray those with whom they appear to have become one. I pray that this will not be my fate, that with what I have written, I have finally found a place for my dislocated feelings and that no harm or hurt will come to those on whom I have relied to remain invisible.

the departures

dad — june 1998

"Yoo-hoo! Yoo-hoo." It's eerie, the way the sound of my father's shouts travels so clearly across the yard, even in the dead of night. Someone's graffitied the word *yoo-hoo* on the garbage can outside his house, and there's a bottle of the chocolate drink in his refrigerator. Some joke. I don't know how my brother can stand it.

Only the flash of Geoff's camera punctures the dimness. He's chronicling Dad's demise, his delirium. It seems pretty warped, this picture-taking of my father's disintegration. Maybe it's some sort of search for permanence, for a record or a connection with the man who deserted him so long ago. It's incredibly strange that we as a family have only one photo album. It's full of those Polaroid shots of our teenage years that are curling around the edges and fading as quickly as they once appeared. Another chapter in our saga of "now you see us; now you don't."

Geoff tells me that it's only a matter of days now. But I don't believe him. And I can't find the courage to reach out and say good-bye. I'm as numb as I was during childbirth. On the last morning I see my father alive, the only gesture that feels less than mechanical is returning his ashtray. "I'm sorry, Dad. I'm sorry I took it," I whisper in his ear. "Do you remember that room at the Hassler. How you loved the view?"

"He was dead when I went in for breakfast at six," Geoff says when he calls early Wednesday morning. "I guess he died around dawn." I had no premonition this time. But I feel another rush of adrenaline, that familiar flurry of frenzied motion that stands in for emotion. When I arrive by taxi in Ridgefield and drop off my bag at Mom's, she's on the phone. "Your brother's in the back," she says.

The hospital bed is already gone. Like the whiteness of the wrist beneath a watchband when you're tanned from the sun, the Kermanshah rug is brighter in the space beneath where his bed has been. *Maybe our lives will be brighter now too,* I think. Staring at the pattern of pink, blue, and violet flowers that suddenly seems to have sprung up from a green as translucent as the sea, I start cleaning.

My father's dead, and I can't stop cleaning — scrubbing down counters, throwing out pill bottles, polishing tables, washing the scum and film off his drinking glasses. I want to get rid of everything: the oxygen bottles, the masks, the tubes, the three-year-old frozen Meals on Wheels. When my brother catches me dumping Hefty bags outside, he's icy with rage. "Don't touch anything. Just leave it alone. I'll do it later."

It must seem heartless, the cleaning up, this last bit of controlling. I can't really blame him. It's Geoff, not me, who's changed my father's sheets and diapers for the past six months, who's come out from his shack to hold his hand and to comfort him. He feels I have no place here, no right to touch or to move Dad's belongings.

When I open Dad's closet and see the pair of L. L. Bean gloves, I finally sit down and cry. These gloves created almost as much drama in our family as the blood-soaked Isotoners O.J. tried on in the courtroom. They were a Christmas gift from Mother, a gentle hint to Dad that he might occasionally enjoy taking a walk outside. He didn't, and the gloves sat in the closet, unworn for years. One weekend, Richard borrowed them to go out in the snow and shovel the driveway. He forgot to put them back. Two days later, I got a message on my machine. "Bastard! Bastard. Glove." Richard sent them up by Airborne Express with a note that said, "I Glove You."

I laughed. We all did. It seemed crazy — that a man who hadn't been outdoors in years should actually care about a pair of gloves. But they were his. They belonged to him. Like the ashtray. I suppose my father felt that enough had been taken from him by then: his speech, his movement, his money, his memory. What a pity he never realized just how much had been given to him.

"Did Pino die of cabin fever, Mom?" asked Jack. "Is that why his temperature was so high?" "Yes," I wanted to shout. "He did. That's exactly what he died of." Cradling my son in my arms and struck by the awe of this truth, I said, "No, not really, Jack. He was tired and old, that's all." This is the closest I come to actual grief. This brief moment with my son.

Geoff has set up an appointment with a guy named Scott at Kane's Funeral Home for the next morning. "Don't call it a goddamn home," Mom yells from the kitchen when I call information for the number to confirm the time of our appointment. "It's a *parlor,* a funeral *parlor.*" That same night, Larry and Deansy hold their own wake on Dad's porch. They're drinking straight tequila and shooting holes in a cardboard box with a .22. Larry's used a Magic Marker to draw a picture of a rat on the flap, in honor of the days when he and Dad would go off to shoot them at the town dump on Sunday afternoons.

Larry's wearing a suit. With the exception of his brief appearance at his daughter's wedding, when, as he told me, he arrived too late to walk her down the aisle and someone at the party had to point her out because he didn't recognize her, Larry hasn't worn a jacket in twenty-five years. He's even unearthed a yellow silk ascot and trimmed his beard.

Kane's is right across the street from St. Mary's Church. There are green-and-white-striped awnings over the windows. But the windows are dark. It's pretty weird, talking to Scott, to this twenty-something kid in Top-Siders and khakis who is overseeing the funeral arrangements. Geoff provides the information that Scott needs in order to make my father's death official: social security number, birth date, pronouncement of death, credit card number. We've decided that Dad won't need a casket. He'll be cremated.

There's something so premature about Scott's gravity; it makes me almost giddy. "Where did you go to school?" I ask him. "What made you choose to be an undertaker?" "Do you have any children?" But my questions only seem to make Scott all the more uncomfortable. This isn't a cocktail party or a job interview. I'm supposed to be bereaved. What Scott doesn't understand is that I'm not bereaved. I'm just in a hurry. Maybe it's shock, this sensation of speed that seems to propel me as quickly through the service at Kane's as it does through the aisles of the supermarket where Rachel and I shop for the lunch afterward.

"Generous but often unkind" is all I remember of the words said by his friend Ronald at the service. That and Geoff's mention of the terrible price my father paid for living life his way. I see faces I haven't seen in years. Women who worked for Dad at Clarks, friends of my mother's, even neighbors who were around back in the days when she sang and shrieked about the heat, wearing nothing but a bra and underpants in the backyard.

In the week that follows the service, when long-lost friends begin to call with condolences from all around the world and reminisce about their years of traveling with Dad, I am astounded to discover how little I really knew about this foreigner I called my father. I never knew about his visit to Dachau, a visit that moved him so profoundly that he cried in the car driving back to Munich. I had never seen my father cry. I never knew about the night two men jumped him outside the Savoia Hotel in Rome, and that he beat them so badly, the concierge had to call an ambulance. (I wish, like his proud friend Hugh Woods who told me this story, that I had seen this as a moment of triumph for my father rather than as a foreshadowing of tragedy.)

I did know that Dad was irresistible to women, even that he'd had affairs. It didn't shock me. I took an almost perverse pride in the ease with which my father seemed to seduce everyone around him. As the only member of the family who knew about them (or so I assumed), I felt privileged. Trusted.

What I never knew until Hugh's phone call was that he

had once fallen so madly in love with a young woman named Flavia that he flew Pan Am #1 to Rome every other Friday for four years to spend a single day with her before reboarding a flight back to New York. Could the ashtray from the Hassler have been a souvenir of that romance with Flavia? Had he held onto that memory all these years without a word? Or did the stroke delete the memory of Flavia the same way it seemed to have deleted so many other memories and emotions?

And what about my mother? Had she always known or suspected that Dad, like our dog Pal, was a rogue male? A philanderer? Is this why she had worn his gold while gardening and flung that diamond wristwatch across the room and hit him in the face? I had always thought the jewelry was a symbol of Dad's success, that there was no excuse for Mother's indifference, for her rejection of a world that meant so much to him and that others envied and admired.

Charm and "a mastery of gesture" is what these men mention most when they call to reminisce about my father. "I'll never forget our last trip to Ireland," Hugh tells me the second night he phones from Toronto. "The head of the union at our buddy's factory dropped dead the day before we arrived. We had to go to the wake. When we got to the house, everybody was piss drunk. They'd been drinking for twenty-four hours. But your father went right up to the host and asked where the body was. To pay his last respects, you know? The guy just guffawed.

"The corpse was sitting straight up in the chair behind him, clutching a beer bottle. They'd dragged him out of his coffin. Your Dad grabbed a Guinness from the kitchen sink, looked the corpse in the eye, and shouted, 'Cheers.' The next morning, he made us all walk behind this 1936 Packard hearse, through town and up the hill to the graveyard."

There was no need for my father to have shown up at that wake or to have escorted the corpse of a man he'd never known to his grave. This was part of what made my father so irresistibly human and seductive, the timing and spontaneity of such gestures. But it was also the seeming effortlessness with which he made them, the fact that he made people feel as if it was his privilege to know and be near them.

Despite the impact of these stories and how vividly they resurrect the ghost of a man I have long ago laid to rest, I can't help but think that for the first half of my life, Dad was away on business. For the second half, it was illness that took him away. I spent years paying off the debt I owed to him when I became his conservator, his protector. I feel no guilt and very little sadness now that he is gone.

But two weeks after the service, I find two small inflated lymph nodes in my neck. I've never felt this kind of weariness. It's a sluggishness that seems to seep into my bones and creep through my entire being. Even my brain feels heavy. It reminds me of the slow-motion feeling I had in the seconds before hitting a stone wall in my father's new BMW years ago. Maybe the body does this on purpose, I think, slows down to give you time to respond. I'm trying to respond to my father's death, to feel it.

My doctor aspirates one of the nodes with a needle and gives me a prescription for antibiotics. The nodes deflate, but on Monday afternoon he calls me at home.

"How are you feeling, Brenda?"

"Pretty good," I say. "I think they're going away."

"Well, I got your results back from the lab."

"Uh-huh. And?"

"They indicate Hodgkin's lymphoma."

I feel like I'm floating, it's so unreal. "Hodgkin's lymphoma?"

"Yes. But listen, the results from aspirations are very often wrong. I'd like to do a biopsy. Take them out."

Jesus. I'm dying. Could this be my punishment for distancing myself from my father in his last years? for wishing he would just go away and die? I am like a small child who assumes that when a wish comes true it is because she made it so. For three days after the operation, I wander around in that limbo of fear and fatigue that always overtakes me before flying. Then the doctor calls my machine at the beach. "I'm not supposed to do this, leave a message on your machine. But you're fine. It was an infection. Call me if you have any questions."

I have a lot of questions. Like what we're going to do with Dad's ashes. Our original plan was to send the ashes up into the swamp in a burning canoe, to give Dad a sort of Viking's funeral. Uncle Larry would shoot the flaming arrow and away he'd go. The canoe, unfortunately, leaked like a sieve. And the swamp, thanks to the dam Dad built to the dismay and fury of our neighbors thirty years ago, was so thick with algae, weeds, and dead tree stumps, it was impassable.

Part of Dad is now on the bottom of the River Arno in Florence. My sister carried over some of his remains in a Baggie and flung them off the Ponte Vecchio. Another part of him is in a Café Bustelo coffee can in her laundry room in Virginia. After Geoff grabbed a handful or two of ashes for himself, he sent the rest down to her via FedEx in a plastic shopping bag.

It sounds inhuman, throwing one's father off a bridge in a Baggie, shipping him around in a FedEx box, and keeping his remains in a coffee can. But I imagine my father chuckling. Not only would he find our difficulties in locating a suitable resting place funny, I think he'd be delighted to know he ended up somewhat scattered — wandering around the after-life with one foot in and one foot out.

If, as the poet Derek Walcott claims, "survival is the triumph of stubbornness," every day since my mother found my father naked on that couch was a triumph for him. Unlike my mother, he never surrendered. In the eighteen years I watched him struggle for everything from words to breath itself, I never heard him once complain of pain. "It's not what you leave behind; it's what you bring with you, Brenda." This is what he'd said to console me that morning I stood sobbing at Orly Airport, three days after we'd shared a bottle of wine at the Meurice and I'd agreed to fly home and meet my family.

The night I arrived in Ridgefield, I sat on the floor in my bedroom while my parents fought downstairs and my brother and sister wept. "It's OK," I said to these siblings who were strangers, to the brother and sister I hadn't really seen or lived with in over ten years. "Don't worry. It's going to be OK. I'm here." I wonder now if my father might have had some sort of premonition then, if he sensed the dead end ahead.

The dead end came long before that night he had the stroke, the same night a local friend of his finally told me that Dad had been beaten in a parking lot outside a bar by Dick Mahoney. (Mahoney was Dad's partner in the real estate development up in New Milford.) It seems someone had been vandalizing the houses up at Parkwood for months. When Dad found out it was Dick who was scratching obscenities on newly installed plate-glass windows, throwing sand into the gas tanks of dump trucks, and defacing the freshly painted Sheetrocked walls, he went nuts.

"No one but your father ever knew why Dick had done it. But I never saw your father that enraged," the friend said. "He hadn't been sleeping or eating for months. He'd sunk every hope and his whole future into that place, you know?"

Today, developers tell me that Parkwood, one of the first group of McMansions ever built in Connecticut, is a gold mine. They tell me that the man who built it was a "visionary," a man who "cut no corners." When I think of my father now, I think of those dream houses, houses that he had to blast out the side of a mountain to create. "Just look at that view, Brenda," he'd said to me, opening his arms in a gesture so wide, it seemed to embrace almost everything around him — from the sun and the sky to all those imaginary people, the families, he saw enjoying his view.

Like that seemingly endless stretch of sun and sky in front of us, my father had no sense of the finite. Maybe this is why he failed with family. We were too small a concept, too small a world, for him to deal with. There was nothing small about my father. Not even in his stingiest, meanest moments.

Of all the notes and messages sent to the family after he died, there is only one that I have kept as a daily reminder of my father's gifts. It is a fax sent from a man named Tom Austin, a man who had worked for him for years. "This memo of your father's became a legend in our industry," Tom scrawled across the bottom of the fax. "I don't know anyone who hasn't either read it or heard about it."

Written by my father to a customer who had refused to pay for several shipments of shoes and dated August 13, 1975, it says:

Dear Obie:
The lovely fall season in New England is only seven or eight weeks away as I write this letter, and the leaves will be changing color in their usual attractive manner. I hope that before the leaves change, you will have sent me a great deal of money.

Cordially,
Robert T. Cullerton

Every time I read that memo, I laugh out loud. I think of my father's humor, of how he worshiped words and how even when he lost them, when they betrayed him, he refused to feel sorry for himself. This is what I choose to remember most vividly about him now — his words. And yes, his wisdom.

mom — august 1998

DESPITE THE SLACK-JAWED, SUNKEN-CHEEKED SLEEP that looks so much like death, there is a part of me that continues to believe in the possibility of Mother making one more rebound. But nurses say her systems are shutting down, and the distance she'd have to travel back now seems almost as vast as the oceans she once loved.

When we were little, Mom rented a house for us up in Kennebunkport, Maine. For five summers, we'd ride our bikes on August afternoons and devour lobster rolls and French fries by the pound. The bleak landscape, the blunt, stone-faced natives, and the cold, inhospitable sea reflected the same darkly defiant regions of the soul she shared with my father but that Dad preferred to wish away in sunnier, more placid places.

As we climbed among the rock pools and filled our buckets with starfish, she'd tell us stories of widows waiting for whaling ships that had been swallowed in "a single gulp" by the sea and of countless other ships that sank: the *Edmund Fitzgerald,* the *Mary Deare,* the *Andrea Doria,* the *Lusitania,* the *Titanic.* "All gone to a watery grave," she'd say almost wistfully as we made our way back home through the rain and fog.

It's amazing how my talk of ships now seems to comfort her. It's all I have to offer her, these memories of sailing beneath the Verrazano Bridge with the shimmer of skyscrapers shrinking into the distance behind me and that first ecstatic glimpse of the uninterrupted sea ahead. "Such release," she says, between spoonfuls of watermelon juice and her Xanax-laced ice cream. "Such release."

My mother is so incredibly light, I wish I could carry her over that threshold of death and into the happy hunting grounds myself — to the destination that after so many years of obsessive dread is no longer quite so far away. "What if they think I'm dead and I'm not?" she'd said that day at the lawyer's months ago. "What if they bury me breathing?"

My mother was buried alive years ago. Suffocated bit by bit by her past and by her fear of joy. So diminished by her mother's indifference and my father's heedlessness, by his unholy neglect of her, that even her books became a kind of tomb. A crypt of words whose walls gradually grew so high and thick around her, no light or outside voice could penetrate the gloom.

But here in this untethered state right before dying, there are moments when she seems to find a kind of peace, a fearlessness. Even her eyes become as blue and clear as the sky we can finally see outside her open window. Perhaps this is the definition of peace for all of us: the absence of fear. But how unspeakably sad, that such lucidity and peace should come to my mother not when she was living but when she is so close to leaving.

At other moments, I can hear her swearing when people touch her. Not with old-fashioned harmless words like *crumbs of Paris* or *Judas priest.* But with the rough, obscene words my father used to wound her: "Fuck, fuck, bastard." It shocks me, to hear them come out from her mouth. For some reason, I keep thinking of that fairy tale — the one about the selfish daughter who spat out toads after refusing to give a drink of water to a poor woman at the town well, and of the other daughter, the kind, unselfish one who spewed out diamonds and roses instead.

Am I that selfish daughter? I wonder. Another of the many heedless ones whose distance so diminished my mother? Is this why I've always thought of myself as the bad seed? How could I have turned away from a woman who yearned only for acknowledgment and the smallest show of affection? a woman who prefaced her every letter to me with "Dearest BBC — love of my life — Firstborn. Princess of princesses — Ave," and who never failed to sign them, "Your devoted mother always, MMcL"?

If only I were more adept at the physical acts of caring, at the changing of sheets and nightgowns, I could show her now. But I'm awkward, nervous. And this is no time for awkwardness. Not when every movement creates such pain. After all the years of running, the slightest shift of bone or muscle now makes my mother whimper.

She whimpers the way Fuss, our German shepherd, did after he got hit chasing a car. The car smashed in his whole left side. I can still see him, listing sideways as if the wind were blowing him over when he tried to walk, and I can hear the keening sound of his cries before he disappeared and died in the woods.

I envy my sister. She seems so still, so perfectly attuned to the moment. "Mommy, Mommy," I hear from the kitchen as I work to keep busy moving. Making endless pots of iced tea and iced coffee, walking, washing dishes, smoking. There isn't a cynical bone in my mother's body, I think, as I watch Rachel and Bernice ever so gently turn her over and slide the sheet out from beneath her. They're taking turns reading out loud to her from a book called *Letting Go.* But Mom is still resisting.

A young Irish priest comes by to anoint her, twice. "Extreme Unction" they used to call it. I try to conjure up the words to the prayers she and I both learned by heart and repeated so many thousands of times at the convent. But I can't. Not even the Our Father or the Hail Mary. So I repeat the names of the nuns instead. These women who for Ma were the only mothers she ever really knew: Mother Cotter, Reverend Mother Fitzgerald, Mother O'Rourke. I'm glad she is dying a believer — not just in God, but in us. Mother was proud of us. She didn't know the first thing about how to take care of us, but she believed in us.

Her fever keeps climbing, and she's coughing. We place cool, wet washcloths at the pulse points: under her arms, around her feet and wrists, and on her forehead. My sister insists on sleeping on the floor of Mom's room and comes up to get me at dawn. "Please come down. She's hysterical."

"You have to sleep, Ma," I say. I'm standing at the foot of her bed. "You're driving Rachel crazy. Just close your eyes and go to sleep."

"I don't know where I'm going," she mutters. "I don't know where I'm going."

"That's all right, Ma," I say. "None of us knows where we're going."

Mother, like everyone else, has always assumed I knew precisely where I was going. And for as long as I kept on going, I did. But this may have been my gift to her. The knowledge, or the illusion, that I am a child who seems to have found a direction, who works with the words she revered, and who is loved by a man as kind as he is witty.

It's Friday night when we begin to hear the sounds of Stan banging. "What the freakin' hell is he doing?" I ask Rachel when I collapse into a chair in the den. "He's been over there pounding for hours."

"I think he's finishing his bridge to the island," says Rachel.

"Our mother's dying, and he's finishing a bridge to the island? Is he crazy?"

But Stan is another of reality's refugees whom Mother has sheltered. *Maybe his hammering and his bridge-building are a way of grieving,* I think to myself before going to bed.

Saturday morning, when we wake up to the sounds of cars honking and parking in the backyard and see the wooden signs for his tag sale, the mystery of the banging is solved. "I'm gonna kill him," I say to Rachel as we sink down into the pillows of the couch in the den, trying to avoid the curious eyes of strangers who peer through the windows. "A fucking tag sale? How dare he?"

"Bren, it's not his fault. He didn't know she was going to die. He ran the ads a week ago. And he did apologize to me. Plus, Stan is Mother's friend."

Rachel's right. This is the way my mother lived her life.

Why shouldn't she die the same way? There's nothing new about seeing this parade of strangers passing through my backyard.

Eric and Geoff are in and out all day. Eric plays the guitar for her. Her best friend, Chris, and Rita Feinson also come to say good-bye, along with the Tobins and Marie. The stink in Mother's room on this last day chokes me. Her eyes are clouding over, and her toes are turning purple. It's been seven days, and still she's holding on.

We catch her seconds before she dies. "Come quick," shouts Pearlie. "She's going." Rachel grabs her hand. She's kneeling by the bed and sobbing. "Mommy, Mommy." I stand close by without touching my mother and see a single tear slide down her face. It's me who stays behind to close her eyes. Why am I so self-conscious? Why can't I think of anything to say as my hand gently brushes over her forehead?

An hour later, Scott from Kane's Funeral Home pulls into the driveway in a jumbo black Suburban. No way my mother is going to have to ride in the back of a 4 x 4. Scott seems timid, tentative, when I open the door. He's probably been out on a date. But he's also carrying something that looks exactly like a black Hefty bag. Oh my God. Pearlie keeps poking her head around the corner of the kitchen door. "Is that the coroner?" she says, giggling. "Is that really him?"

"No, Pearlie. It's the undertaker."

The three of us, Geoff, Rachel, and I, sit in the den, while Scott and his helper are in Mother's room. We're laughing. "Shhh," I keep saying. "What if he hears us?" But I'm sure Scott has heard worse than this in his years picking up the dead. It is unimaginable, what he must be doing in that room.

I refuse to get up. I am afraid to move for fear of catching him in the act of carrying my mother out of her house in a heavy-duty garbage bag. Why can't they use a shroud or a gurney?

There's a moment when I clap my hand over my mouth to quiet the echo of Mom's voice. I can hear the sound of her shrill command to everyone from exterminators and plumbers to houseguests. "Don't forget to take out the garbage," she'd yell while reading on her bed. When I hear the crunch of gravel as Scott peals out of the driveway, I have this vision of her sitting straight up in that bag in the backseat and shaking her fists. Just like she did in the old days. "Slow down, you slob, you show-off," she'd scream at the end of the driveway. "There are children playing here."

We bury Mom on Monday at the Danbury Cemetery. I'd have liked to arrange for rain and hurricane winds. But the sun is out. Her grave is within eyesight of the hill where Grandma Marie's old house once stood, a house she loved, and of a headstone that marks the grave of the laundress, Mrs. Gerow. We've asked for a plain pine box, a casket like Dickens's paupers. *Nothing nouveau,* I remember thinking to myself. *Nothing ostentatious.*

Her parents, Arnold and Mary, are next to her in unmarked graves. After all the years of Mother talking about the McLachlans and the hat capital of the world, there is no sign that anyone has remembered them. I'm astounded at this blankness, at their anonymity. How could these somebodies have been buried like nobodies? Standing with my brother and sister next to what looks like a gray felt box, I am unable to find much comfort in the words of the priest or in the company of the few who are here with us.

I feel my mother's terror of the dirt and the darkness as they lower the box into the ground. She's wearing her favorite Lanz nightgown, her pink bathrobe, and a pair of fuzzy pink slippers. I even gave Scott a handkerchief for her to hold and a bandanna for her hair.

Parking the car at St. Mary's before the church service, I suddenly realize that I haven't been here since I was a child, not since the days when Mom used to pull in on Sunday mornings, open the door, and shove us out of the car for Sunday school and church. But both of my feet are on the ground this time, and I'm not running. I'm walking. As I fidget in my pew, I'm grateful for the words spoken by her dearest friend, Chris.

"Mary's boredom with the prosaic details of life was as vast as her tolerance of fools was nil," she says with a smile. "She saddened me beyond words when I couldn't help her as her illness stole away her hope. But then a miracle happened — she became more serene than I had ever known her. The love in that bedroom of hers in those last days was palpable. She loved us all and we loved her, and it seemed to me that in these things, in the end, she finally found her heart's desire."

The day after the service, there are still a few stragglers, last-minute shoppers passing through the backyard. A friend of Marie's arrives with a bouquet of wildflowers: black-eyed Susans, daisies, Queen Anne's lace. "Your mother was a warrior," she says. "A wonderful woman." The fact that she then wanders off to rifle through the little that is left of Stan's bargains only makes me smile. *Mom would love this,* I think, before carrying the flowers back into the house and dumping them in the garbage. They're full of tiny little bugs, the black-eyed Susans. And they suck up all the oxygen.

the house — january 1999

I CANNOT BELIEVE THAT THE NAME OF THE COUPLE WHO are about to invade my backyard and occupy my mother's house is Cronewart. It's a name straight out of one of Mother's favorite Dickens novels. Better than Mr. Gradgrind or Uriah Heep. I'm sitting in their lawyer's office in Ridgefield, looking at the two-page closing statement for the house. Considering just how long and tortuous the journey has been to get here, the statement seems ridiculously short. What if these people could read between the lines?

No way you'll ever belong there, I think to myself as I sneak furtive glances at Mrs. Cronewart, at this usurper dressed in her perfectly creased khakis with her chic disheveled gray hair and her red velvet headband. Her story about a son who's called to tell her he's skipped work because he forgot his favorite Paul Stewart blazer and Mont Blanc pen at home would have made my parents nauseated. "I've always preferred my Bic," I say with a snicker before signing on the solid line.

In the months immediately following my mother's death, I feel as if I've woken up inside one of those cocoons of angel hair, as if there are tiny filaments of glass embedded in my skin. Everything that has to do with life irritates me. I hurt. I am so thin, I keep thinking I must be transparent. And I wonder why no one can see through me.

The devastation at the house is so complete, the years of neglect so obvious, I figure we'll be lucky if we can give it away. Some fool has pruned the lilac bushes too far back. You can see how deep the roots have dug themselves into the foundation. Reading the engineer's report is a nightmare. Between the radon and bacteria in the well and in the basement, the termites "devouring" the beams, the rotting windows, and the rusted-out oil tank, I'm amazed my mother lived as long as she did. The infestation of raccoons, squirrels, and other "unknown wildlife" in the attic is so "impressive," the engineer suggests we hire a zookeeper to remove them.

No wonder the house isn't "showing very well," as the Realtor diplomatically puts it. "But don't lose heart," he says. "You only need one buyer."

"You might also consider removing some of the personal touches," he adds, pointing to the refrigerator. The refrigerator is where Mother kept track of people who unwittingly froze, drowned, and burned to death going outside. My sister and I spend a weekend pulling her cartoons and the newspaper clippings off the icebox and hiding the McLachlan family photographs in the garage. Steve Tobin comes over from across the street to tear down the wall.

I'm going to miss the Tobins. Steven, James, John, and Larry are the last of the locals, "indigenous peoples," in a town overrun by new and nameless hordes of corporate nomads. For me, the Tobins will always be "somebodies," not just because their great-grandfather was a Rockwell, as Mom liked to tell us, but because they loved my mother and showed such respect for my father, and because they have always been so remarkably loyal and discreet.

Steven does such a meticulous job tearing down the wall and refinishing the steps, it's hard to believe it was ever there at all. The Realtor is delighted. But looking at his finished brochure is like stepping into some episode of the *Twilight Zone.* This isn't my house with "its cozy country kitchen made for happy family dinners" and "living room rich in history with lovely beehive oven." He's swiped words from Mother's obituary to advertise the view of the backyard. "Creative inspiration," he called it. "Once one of the most popular rural scenes in town for local artists and photographers," it boasts. Who does he think he's kidding?

There has been such a radical altering of the physical geography of that backyard that I no longer recognize it. My father's house is gone. It took a backhoe twenty minutes to raze it. Getting rid of it was part of a deal we made when we sold the lot to a local developer three months before Mother died. (An optimistic impulse aimed at generating cash for her future.) He plans to build a 1.4-million-dollar "tract" house, a McMansion, on it.

In the meantime, twisted gas pipes stick up out of the dirt, and there are bits of metal and shattered glass and chunks of broken concrete everywhere. The cast-iron stove that warmed the living room is sitting all by itself out on the lawn. The doors have rusted shut. I see the square of dirty green linoleum where the kitchen was, where Dad made his peanut-butter-and-jelly sandwiches.

There's also a twelve-foot pile of rocks in the middle of the meadow and a trench running through the thicket where Grandma's raspberry bushes once grew. I find myself desperately searching for landmarks, for something to hold on to. But even the limbs of the apple tree my kids climbed on weekends are gone.

As the months pass and the skeleton of the McMansion begins to rise from the slush and the snow, I think of Mother in her grave, a grave that despite our talk of headstones and epitaphs remains unmarked. Unvisited. Perhaps it's Mother's spirit that sends me out one afternoon to surreptitiously pull up and move the surveyor's posts back an inch or two. It's an act of sabotage that I know she would approve of.

"I'm building a model home here," the developer proudly tells me when he passes by one Sunday afternoon. "Just like the ones down on Hutchins Close." God. How I've always loved that expression. Who comes from a "model home," anyway? And what is it with these new words like *close* and *lane?* Are they supposed to imply an old-fashioned sense of intimacy? of safety?

With the exception of slight differences in facade, every one of these houses features the same four bedrooms, including master suite with marbled bath and Jacuzzi, modern "colonial" kitchens, and four-car garages. They are identical. And they're built in "clusters," within easy shouting distance of one another. Yet despite this suffocating proximity, I'm told that most of these people will pay to install invisible fencing.

"Sadists!" my mother would have screamed. "Depraved

sadists!" But what a sublime metaphor, these invisible fences, for the lives of those who install them, for vigilantly guarded, oh-so-small worlds and for the fears and the terrors that must lurk beneath this shriek for sameness, for containment. Do these people experience the same shock as their pets do when they venture out of their backyards? when they leave familiar boundaries behind?

I am as fascinated as I am repulsed by this taming of the wild. If this is the price one pays for belonging (and I'm not talking about the 1.4 million dollars), I will never be able to afford it. Because there seems to be room in these people's lives and in their new houses for everything but the imagination. "Fear," my mother once told me, "is the curse of a great imagination." I think of that on my final walk through Mother's house. A house that I refer to as "De Void." Stripped of everything but its scars and cracks, its gaping wounds, it no longer seems quite so haunted. Just empty. For some reason, I can't imagine either leaving this house or ever returning to it. Then I remember the call from the Danbury Police two weeks after Mother died.

My aunt Janet had shown up for dinner at the old house in Danbury on Ohehyahtah Place — the house she and Mother had grown up in. She was drunk. "I'm home," she announced to the two bewildered strangers who stood gaping at this tiny geriatric intruder at the top of their cellar stairs. "Tell Daddy I'm sorry I'm late."

Late? How 'bout thirty-five years late? What is it that had led my aunt back to a house in which she, like my mother, had experienced so much horror and unhappiness? Was it a need to somehow retrieve what had been lost long before she left?

Was it loneliness, or a desire to finally heal the wounds and seal the cracks? "Cracks are made to let the light in," Geoff told me the day before we buried Mother.

Like my mother, I'm afraid of the light. I'm afraid it will expose the cracks, the faults that run like fissures just below my surface. Without my facade, I too may become unhinged and helpless. Perhaps this is what my fears, my terrors, of the void are really about. Not death, but helplessness.

I did not come from a place that even remotely resembled a model home. Nothing about my parents' lives or their deaths was neat or tidy. Everything was extreme, blown way out of proportion. But, my God, how unbearably alive and hugely human they were!

Somewhere in the midst of the humanity and helplessness, I know there is hope. I know this because when I read out loud to my daughter, Nora, from the same chapter in *The Wind in the Willows* that once had my mother stifling sobs, I am also crying. Called "Dulce Domum," it's the chapter in which Mole and his friend Ratty are returning from a visit to Badger's house in the Wild Wood. Hurrying through the snow, tired and cold, Mole is stunned by the smell, the tug, of something strangely familiar. The harder he struggles to free himself from its hold, the stronger it becomes. Finally, he sits down by the side of the road and cries.

> "I know it's a — shabby, dingy little place," he sobbed forth, brokenly, "not like — your cozy quarters — or Toad's beautiful hall — or Badger's great house — but it was my own little home — and I was fond of it —

and I went away and forgot all about it — and then I smelt it — on the road — and everything came back to me in a rush — and I wanted it! Oh dear, oh dear! We might have just gone back and had one look at it, Ratty. It was close. But you wouldn't turn back, Ratty. You wouldn't turn back."

On the drive from Ridgefield to New York, I am on a road that is such a part of me, I can anticipate its every hill, curve, and straightaway, a road I have traveled so many times, I know it can't possibly hold any surprises. Yet it suddenly seems unfamiliar. I feel as if I have been ambushed. I am agonizingly alert to its every bump, to every change in sound, even as the wheels move from one kind of tar to another. This is a new, unknown road. It is the road that is leading me away for the very last time from the place where I began. My palms are sweaty, and my heart is racing. Peering desperately out into the darkness, I am terrified I will miss the exit, the exit that marks the way home. That's me, still terrified of missing the exit but happy to be going home.

a family update: september 2002

My brother, Geoff, currently lives in a house "bigger than the Taj Mahal" in China, where he is running one of the largest shoe factories in the People's Republic. His pinkie fingernail is longer than that of the former dowager empress, and he speaks nearly fluent Mandarin.

My seventy-five-year-old uncle, Larry, suffered a massive heart attack while partying in Maine. He was medevacked out to a hospital in Connecticut and had a quintuple bypass. Last we heard, he was heading south in a van to yet another bluegrass dance marathon.

The McMansion behind my mother's house is finished, inhabited, and surrounded by invisible fencing. It is so huge, people who pass by assume that Mom's house belongs to the caretaker.

My beloved aunt Janet died in June and is buried next to my mother at St. Joseph's Cemetery in Danbury. Thanks to my sister, both graves are marked with headstones.

Gordon, our man from Ghana, now works for friends of ours in Greenwich. He no longer carries a machete or walks barefoot and is the proud father of three children. I see him every other month or so.

author's note

I have changed the names of several persons in this book. The fictitious names are: Stan, Dick Mahoney, Teeny Thorpe, Steven Hadley, Dr. John Brooke, the DiMarco family, the Cronewarts, and my mother's friend and cleaning woman, Susan Murphy. Oh, and there is no such corporation as ConstaCare. The real name is even more hideous.

about the author

Brenda Cullerton lives in New York City with her husband and two children.